W9-CLM-037

SMART Recovery®

Family & Friends

Handbook

for people affected by the
addictive behavior of a loved one

Published by

Alcohol & Drug Abuse Self-Help Network, Inc.
d.b.a. SMART Recovery®
Email: information@smartrecovery.org
www.smartrecovery.org

© 2012 SMART Recovery® - All Rights Reserved

On a daily basis, the SMART Recovery® Central Office receives phone calls from family members and friends of someone who is struggling with addiction. These mothers, fathers, sisters, brothers, partners and friends are looking for ways they can support their Loved One (LO) toward recovery. Their stories make it abundantly clear that they too, feel the negative effects of substance abuse.

SMART began online meetings for Family & Friends (F&F) in 2010. The meetings have two goals: 1) providing self-management and life-skills tools to those struggling with the challenges of living with, and caring about, a LO who has an addiction; 2) supporting F&F in their goal of interacting with their LOs in ways that would maximize the possibility that their LOs would choose recovery.

In our meetings over the last two years, we have refined the SMART tools which we have found to be the most helpful for Family & Friends and have made them available in this Handbook.

Our online F&F members were the inspiration for this publication. We are grateful to them for their many insightful and supportive contributions to our weekly meetings and our message board.

We are also especially grateful to Dr. Robert J. Meyers for the gift of his time, his encouragement, and his scientifically validated methods for interacting with a LO in a helpful way, as outlined in his book *"Get Your Loved One Sober: Alternatives to Nagging, Pleading and Threatening"*.

Another significant contributor to this Handbook was SMART Recovery Australia and the *"Be SMART Manual"*, created for use in the Be SMART: Family & Carers' Program.

There are several individuals without whose help and support our online Family & Friends program would not have been possible. They are: Tom Horvath, President, SMART Recovery, SMART's Executive Director, Shari Allwood, and online facilitators "TwoPutts" and "MomRox" (SMART online pseudonyms) who contributed their knowledge and time (hundreds of hours) planning and facilitating online meetings.

We are excited to announce, with the publication of this Handbook, the expansion of SMART for Family & Friends into the "face-to-face" world. In early 2012, the first face-to-face meeting for F&F was held in Columbia, MD. This meeting was facilitated by Carla N. Miller and Hugh F. Delaney. Shortly thereafter, two more meetings were started: one in San Diego, facilitated by Ashley E. Phillips and one in Chicago, facilitated by Kurt Mohning and Patrick Garnett. We salute these ambitious and dedicated volunteers for initiating SMART meetings for Family & Friends in the United States. We are also grateful to them for reviewing and "testing" this publication.

We hope you, as Family & Friends, will find this Handbook to be a valuable aid as you work to manage the effects of addiction in your life, and to influence your Loved One to pursue recovery.

Roxanne Allen
Editor, SMART Recovery Family & Friends Handbook

About SMART Recovery® for Family & Friends

SMART Recovery® for Family & Friends (F&F) provides support and tools for people who are affected by the addictive behavior of someone close to them. The program aims to help participants develop more effective coping strategies and find a greater sense of fulfilment in their own lives.

This program has been adapted from SMART Recovery® (SMART), and from CRAFT (Community Reinforcement and Family Training) as described in the book *Get Your Loved One Sober: Alternatives to Nagging, Pleading and Threatening*.

SMART is a skills-based, self-help program for individuals struggling with dependencies of all kinds. An alternative to 12-step models such as Alcoholics Anonymous, SMART Recovery uses well-established techniques from modern psychology to equip people with practical skills and tools to overcome any sort of "maladaptive behaviors", from addiction to unhelpful responses to someone else's addiction.

CRAFT is an evidence-based program designed to teach Family & Friends new ways of interacting with a person who has an addiction, with a goal of increasing the chances that the person will seek recovery.

The F&F program has used the four key points of SMART Recovery, and adapted these to suit the needs of family and friends of people with a substance or behavioral addiction.

These four points are as follows:

1. Building and maintaining motivation

2. Coping with urges

3. Managing thoughts, feelings and behaviors

4. Living a balanced lifestyle

The program recognizes that being in a close relationship with someone struggling with an addiction can be a frustrating, painful and sometimes lonely journey, in which it is easy to lose one's bearings.

Rather than focusing on their Loved One, the F&F program invites participants to spend some time concentrating on themselves and their goals, an area they may have been neglecting for some time. This includes looking at some of their habitual responses to their Loved One, exploring whether these are helpful or not, and providing tools and strategies for making changes.

SMART Family & Friends explores ways that participants can look after themselves better, even in difficult and stressful circumstances, and establish healthier relationships with their Loved One.

Taking steps to make changes in life requires considerable courage. Participating in a supportive group environment, comprised of people sharing similar experiences, will hopefully lessen feelings of isolation and instill a sense of hope.

Self-Management & Recovery Training (SMART) for Family & Friends

How this program helps Family & Friends

SMART for Family & Friends (F&F) is first and foremost a Self-Management program. As a Family or Friend of someone with an addiction it is common to develop a variety of unhelpful habits in response to the addiction: nagging, pleading, threatening, self-medicating with food or other substances, weak or non-existent boundaries. You may have also developed unhelpful ways of thinking leading to anxiety, obsessive thoughts, depression and anger management problems/challenges. Even though your wish is likely to support your Loved One (LO) toward recovery, your own well-being could be suffering as you attempt to do so. The SMART tools offered in this handbook can support you in finding ways to restore emotional and behavioral balance in your life so that you can calmly and effectively deal with the challenges you face.

SMART F&F also supports you in learning ways to be as supportive as possible of your LO by exploring the skills and strategies outlined in the book *Get Your Loved One Sober* (GYLOS). Many of these skills and strategies are reviewed in this handbook.

Acronyms used in this handbook

CRAFT: Community Reinforcement and Family Training
CSO: Concerned Significant Other (of someone with addiction)
F&F: Family & Friends (of someone with addiction)
GYLOS: The book "Get Your Loved One Sober: Alternatives to Nagging, Pleading and Threatening"
LO: Loved One (someone with addiction or in recovery)

Using this handbook

This handbook is designed to be used by an individual alone or in a SMART meeting for F&F.

Meetings for Family & Friends

SMART Recovery meetings are a safe place to meet with others who have similar concerns, talk about the challenges you face and to learn new skills. Our meetings are solution-oriented (vs. problem-oriented). Most people like the laid-back conversation, the genuine concern people show to others and the non-confrontational, supportive atmosphere.

For information about online and face-to-face meetings please visit the SMART Recovery website: www.smartrecovery.org/family. Our Meeting Guidelines and Meeting Opening are provided on the following pages.

Professional Help

This program is should not be construed as professional therapy. If you are having serious difficulties managing your relationship with your Loved One, we highly recommend that you seek professional help in addition to using the SMART Recovery Program for Family & Friends.

SMART Family & Friends Meeting Guidelines

The focus of SMART Family & Friends is on you and your life, rather than on your Loved One (LO). We are not here to analyze, dissect or try to change your Loved One's problematic behavior. Instead, we will be inviting *you* to concentrate on *your responses* to their behavior.

Your Loved Ones may be concerned about how you will represent them in this meeting. This meeting is about YOU. Regular SMART meetings address your LO's issues. Both meetings are about how to the use SMART tools to manage the SELF. If you have any questions or concerns about this, please speak with the facilitator after the meeting.

The group membership and what is said in the group is to remain confidential. Please do not discuss who you saw here or what was said with anyone outside of the group. Confidentiality helps to create an atmosphere of safety and privacy for our members. Note: Some facilitators staff both F&F and regular SMART Recovery meetings. Be assured that the facilitator holds your participation and comments about your LO in confidence and will not divulge that information outside of this meeting. Similarly, the facilitator will not divulge information about your LO in this meeting.

Treat other group participants with respect. Although you may not necessarily agree with everything everyone says, they are entitled to their opinion. Try not to label, judge or put down other group participants. This includes your LO (whether or not he or she is present)! Try to listen with an open mind. "Respect", "Honesty" and "Understanding" are the bywords for this meeting.

Participate as actively as you like. You are welcome to ask questions and share ideas or just listen. Please be mindful of time and allowing others space to participate.

Allow one person to speak at a time. Listening and being heard is essential to getting the most out of the group experience, so we ask that you not interrupt or have side conversations when one person is speaking. Follow up questions and on-topic conversation are welcome.

Stay focused on SMART Family & Friends. You are more than welcome to try other programs. However, while engaged in this group, you are asked to focus on the SMART material.

The group will start and finish on time. We appreciate your efforts to be here in time for the start of the meeting.

Meeting Opening Statement

Welcome to tonight's SMART Recovery® meeting for Family & Friends.

As some of you may already know, the word SMART stands for Self-Management and Recovery Training. Our meetings are scheduled to run for 90 minutes and should not be construed as professional therapy. Our discussions are open to everyone.

SMART is dedicated to helping individuals gain independence from addictive behavior. Some experts consider addiction to be a disease, some do not. SMART Recovery tools can help you regardless of whether or not you believe addiction is a disease. At SMART we focus on the impact the addiction is having on your life and how you choose to respond.

We believe that although people may have a problematic habit, they are more than just this habit so we do not encourage the use of labels, such as diseased, alcoholic, addict or co-dependent.

We also do not ask you to declare yourself or your Loved One "powerless" over addiction. Instead we ask you to *"discover the power of choice!"* We believe that by focusing on your own thoughts, feelings and behavior you can make your own life more manageable. While there are no guarantees, you may find that changing your behaviors has a positive effect on your Loved One.

Everyone agrees that successful recovery requires making good choices. The solution is SELF...and MANAGEMENT!

SMART is a program based on cognitive therapy methods that provides a "toolbox" designed to allow you to take back control of your life. We provide a supportive network, while you develop the skills for lasting change.

We ask you to be patient with yourself, but persistent. It takes time to change beliefs and develop new ways of behaving around your Loved One, so you will often hear us refer to the 3P's: Practice, Patience and Persistence (PPP).

Respect, Honesty and Understanding are the bywords in this meeting.

Our mutual desire is that your Loved One will take on the choice to pursue their own recovery and that you will learn ways of improving your own life.

We encourage you to attend meetings for as long as they are helpful. In our meetings you will find people in all stages of recovery. As no two meetings are ever alike, do try to come to a few before you decide how helpful SMART can be for you.

We don't charge anything for attendance at these meetings, but a hat will be passed for donations. Donations are requested to offset expenses and to help us to make more meetings available. We're grateful for your support.

Thank you all for being here and we look forward to your participation to make this a great meeting.

Contents

Change and Motivation

The addictive behavior of someone you are close to can have an enormous impact on your emotional and physical well-being. It can be like living on a roller coaster, putting huge pressure and stress on your ability to cope.

If you have "tried everything" and nothing is working, you may have already decided that it's time for *something* to change.

Whether you are looking to support a Loved One toward a positive lifestyle change, whether you are looking to restore some balance to your own life, or whether you are looking to accomplish both, this section will help you to understand *how we change* and *why we change.*

Why Should I Change?

The addictive behavior of someone you are close to can have an enormous impact on your own well-being. It can be like living on a roller coaster, putting huge pressure and stress on your or your family's ability to cope.

You have probably tried lots of different ways to manage the situation and help your Loved One (LO). However, some of these strategies may be wearing you out and actually reducing your ability to cope. Without meaning to, these strategies may also have hindered your LO from facing the consequences of their actions and therefore reduced their motivation to change.

Some examples of the unhelpful coping strategies we are referring to include:

- **Keeping your LO's behavior secret from family and friends** – thereby isolating yourself and denying you a source of potential support.

- **Covering for or "protecting" your LO** – e.g., calling his boss when he is too hung over to go to work the next morning and telling a "white lie"; being her alarm clock on "the morning after" and waking her in time to go to work.

- **Becoming a nurse** – e.g., cleaning up after your LO when he has vomited all over himself and tucking him into bed.

- **Being controlling** – e.g., trying to physically stop your LO from using by doing things like flushing drugs down the toilet, pouring alcohol down the sink, or physically restraining her in some way.

- **Supplying your LO to "keep her safe"** – e.g., buying your LO drugs or alcohol to have at home so that she doesn't go out and get into trouble.

- **"Nagging"** – telling your LO over and over how terrible/destructive his behavior is and that he needs to stop.

- **Pleading with your LO to stop using** – especially when she is under the influence of drugs and/or alcohol and therefore not in a rational frame of mind.

- **Trying harder** – to be a better parent/partner/friend. Exhausting yourself by trying to be more giving and more understanding, often out of a sense of responsibility or guilt.

- **Obsessing over the addictive behavior** – continually thinking about your LO, leaving no time for thinking about your own needs or those of other family members.

- **"Rescuing" your LO when things get tough** – e.g., giving him money when he has run out due to his drug and/or alcohol use.

© 2012 SMART Recovery® - All Rights Reserved Section I: Change and Motivation

Are Your Coping and Helping Behaviors Working?

1. Think of some examples of what you have done to try to cope with the situation and get your Loved One (LO) to stop using. You can write them in the space below.

2. Reflect on what has and what hasn't worked from the above list.

3. Discussion point:

The only behaviors you can control are yours. Setting clear boundaries, respecting yourself and focusing on your own life enables you to stay sane and cope better. It also allows your LO to experience the consequences of his actions and make informed choices for himself. Which of your behaviors in response to your LO's addiction do you think you might want to change?

Set clear boundaries —
Respect myself - my needs!   Be clear on
                              what I need
                              why articulate
                              with kindness

"Things do not change; we change" ~Henry David Thoreau

    © 2012 SMART Recovery® - All Rights Reserved

The Stages of Change

Change is a process, not an event. It usually doesn't happen overnight and it may take effort to achieve. Although making changes may involve some hard work, it will hopefully result in making life more manageable.

Psychologists have identified five stages that people go through when making changes. These stages can help to gain an insight into where you are in relation to making a change.

Stages of Change for Family & Friends

Pre-contemplation

This stage is sometimes termed "denial". You may be completely focused on trying to change the behavior of your Loved One (LO) and are unaware of any reason to change your own behavior. You may feel like you are in complete control of the situation.

Contemplation

You are beginning to reflect on your responses to your Loved One and wonder if they are really helpful. You start to question some of your behaviors and explore some alternatives.

Preparation

You have reflected on your behavior and your responses to your LO and have decided that these are not helpful. You have decided that you want to change. You begin developing new strategies, thinkig about connecting with supportive people, setting goals and making plans.

Action

At this stage you are putting your plans into effect. You are evaluating your new behaviors and observing what is working well and what is not working so well. You are actively working toward goals you have set for yourself.

Maintenance

Things don't seem so difficult any more. Making helpful decisions is becoming more intuitive and you are beginning to see the benefits of the changes you have made.

Sometimes, despite best intentions, you slip back into old ways of responding. We call this a **lapse/relapse** when this happens. This is quite normal and can be part of the process. It's important not to beat yourself up, but to learn from your mistakes and get back on track.

Note: people do not necessarily move between these changes in a straightforward way. They often move forwards and backwards through these stages. It can be helpful to think of the change process as a spiral rather than a straight line.

© 2012 SMART Recovery® - All Rights Reserved

Exercise – Change Motivation Assessment

1. How do you feel about changing your behavior?

On the line below, mark where you think you are on the scale of change readiness:

Not considering change					Thinking about changing					Already changing
0	1	2	3	4	5	6	7	8	9	10

2. What would help you move forward? It might be as simple as "Keep coming to SMART F&F meetings". The space below is for you to list any ideas you have.

3. Importance vs. Confidence.

In order to make a change, it's not only necessary to think that change is important, you also need to feel confident about being able to change.

On the line below, mark **how important** you think it is to change.

Not important										Very important
0	1	2	3	4	5	6	7	8	9	10

On the line below, mark **how confident** you feel about being able to change.

Not confident										Very confident
0	1	2	3	4	5	6	7	8	9	10

"When we are no longer able to change a situation,
we are challenged to change ourselves" ~Viktor Frankl

© 2012 SMART Recovery® - All Rights Reserved

Cost Benefit Analysis (CBA): Weighing the Pros & Cons

Choose a way of responding to your Loved One (e.g., yelling, avoiding, nagging) that you are thinking about changing. Make it specific, for example: *waking my partner after (s)he's been up partying all night so that (s)he doesn't oversleep and miss work.*

- List all the **advantages** of continuing that behavior and all the **disadvantages** of continuing that behavior.

- Then do the reverse: that is, list all the **advantages** of ceasing that behavior and all the disadvantages of ceasing the behavior.

- It can help to label each item either short-term or long-term.

Continuing the Behavior	
Advantages (benefits & rewards)	**Disadvantages (costs & risks)**

Ceasing the Behavior	
Advantages (benefits & rewards)	**Disadvantages (costs & risks)**

The CBA can be used to increase motivation for making behavior changes. Notice that often our current habitual behaviors have short-term benefits, but long-term negative consequences and our new behaviour choices may feel uncomfortable at first, but have long lasting benefits.

Change Plan Worksheet

Planning is a key to making successful changes. Use this worksheet to develop your own plan for making a change in your behavior.

1. The change I want to make is:

2. The most important reasons why I want to make this change are:

3. The steps I plan to take in making this change are:

4. The ways other people can help me are:

    Person: Possible ways to help me:

5. I will know that my plan is working if:

6. Some things that could interfere with my plans are:

7. How important is it that I make this change:

Not important										Very important
0	1	2	3	4	5	6	7	8	9	10

8. How confident am I that I can make this change?

Not confident										Very confident
0	1	2	3	4	5	6	7	8	9	10

  © 2012 SMART Recovery® - All Rights Reserved

Additional Resources

SMART Handbook: Item #1 listed under Best Sellers, on the right hand sidebar in the SMART Recovery Online Bookstore

SMART Quick Start CD: Item #4 listed under Best Sellers, on right hand sidebar in the SMART Recovery Online Bookstore Provides a selection of the Best of SMART Online.

Book: *"Get Your Loved One Sober: Alternatives to Nagging, Pleading and Threatening" (GYLOS)* by Robert J. Meyrs, Ph.D. and Brenda L. Wolfe, Ph.D. Based on Community Reinforcement and Family Training (CRAFT)

Book: "Beyond Addiction, How Science and Kindness Help People Change" by Jeffrey Foote, Carrie Wilkens, and Nicole Kosanke

Book: *"Everything Changes"* by Beverly Conyers For families of those in recovery

NOTES

Self-Care & Self-Rewards

Addiction has a way of quickly throwing lives out of balance. Ask yourself the following questions:

Are you obsessing over your Loved One's addiction and feeling confused and helpless?

Are you finding it hard to get anything done?

Are you having difficulty staying focused on anything else in your life?

Are you reluctant to make plans to do anything, because you never know when "the other shoe is going to drop"?

Are you finding that you're neglecting some important responsibilities because you're distracted and overwhelmed by "the big problem"?

Many Family & Friends answer one or more of the above questions with a "yes."

This section provides tools for assessing your current levels of emotional distress and tools to help you restore balance to your life....the balance you need in order to calmly and effectively manage the challenges you face.

Where Are You on the Emotional Spectrum?

Despair										Hope
0	1	2	3	4	5	6	7	8	(9) 10/24	10

Lonely										Connected
0	1	2	3	4	5	6	7	8	(9) 10/24	10

Dread/Fear										Safe
0	1	2	3	4	5	6	7	(8) 10/24	9	10

Helpless										Empowered
0	1	2	3	4	5	6	7	8	(9) 10/24	10

Anxious										Calm
0	1	2	3	4	5	6	7	(8) 10/24	9	10

Frustrated										Satisfied
0	1	2	3	4	5	6	7	(8) 10/24/22	9	10

Exhausted										Motivated
0	1	2	3	4	5	6	7	(8) 10/24/22	9	10

CRAFT therapists use scales similar to these to measure the progress of Family & Friends who come in for therapy.

Keeping a record of your own emotional assessment scales will allow you to monitor how your emotional well-being changes over time. Consider recording your scales in a journal. Looking back and comparing where you are today with where you were when you started, can be a great motivator. This is especially true when you hit one of those periods when it seems like nothing you're doing is making a difference.

> *"If there is one overriding 'fact' in the world of behavior change, it is that people who record important information about their lives are the people most likely to succeed in making important changes in their lives."* ~GYLOS

© 2012 SMART Recovery® - All Rights Reserved

Oxygen Mask Rule for Family & Friends

Every time we fly, we hear flight attendants sharing some variation of the Oxygen Mask Rule:

"Should the cabin lose pressure, oxygen masks will drop from the overhead area. Please place the mask over your own mouth and nose *before* assisting others."

Why do they say that? What could possibly be wrong with helping others first?

In the case of the airplane, oxygen masks are deployed in situations where the oxygen level has dropped dangerously low. Without our oxygen mask, we will quickly lose consciousness. If we don't make putting on our mask our first priority, we will very likely *not be able to help anyone*.

If someone we love has an addiction that is creating problems, it's natural to want to be a part of the solution. As a result, we may find ourselves devoting abundant energy to the addiction in various ways (educating ourselves about addiction, trying to keep the peace with our Loved One, worrying about the future, trying to influence our Loved One to address the problem). We may choose to do this willingly and lovingly....but in many cases, our choice may come at an expense to our own physical and mental health.

When "helping" (whatever that means in our situation) seems to leave little time for anything else, the result is quite often "burnout". Some feelings that may accompany "giving too much" are exhaustion, frustration, and anger, along with possibly feeling ineffective, helpless, or hopeless.

Rational Emotive Behavior Therapy (REBT) teaches that we are each responsible for our own happiness. When we find ourselves in a situation where our happiness is suffering, the "oxygen mask" analogy is helpful.

To avoid burnout, managing our self-care is a key responsibility to maintain our happiness, our physical health, and our mental health. It requires consciously planning to include time in our day to attend to our *own needs* and make that time a *priority*. If we don't, we eventually *won't* be able to care for others.

What do we really need to maintain our physical and mental health? Exercise, good nutrition, alone time, social time, time for creative endeavors, medical care, and support groups are just a few ideas to consider. We may have become so accustomed to "dealing with" the addiction or trying to "help" our Loved One, that it may feel wrong to give priority to our own needs — but doing so is critical. If we don't take care of ourselves, who will?

Airplanes have sensors to protect against oxygen deprivation. Fortunately, so do we: our friends, relatives, and support group members. We do well to pay attention when we hear others reminding us to *"take care of you first"* or reminding us of the *Oxygen Mask Rule*. They are seeing signs of "oxygen deprivation" in our life, signs that we have not noticed ourselves.

© 2012 SMART Recovery® - All Rights Reserved

The Importance of Self-Care

Being close to someone who has addictive behaviors can be very stressful. You may respond to the stress by doing more and more to try to "fix" the situation, often at the expense of your own needs. Unfortunately, this can lead to you becoming run down and exhausted.

If you are not looking after your own needs and finding some balance in your life it can be difficult to help anyone else or look after your family. You may find yourself dealing with extreme emotions (e.g., depression, anger, burnout). Therefore, it is important to take some time out to look after yourself. It's not selfish, it's selfCARE.

Incorporating self-care into your life

Make daily self-care a top priority
Look after your health, your fitness and your appearance
Actively plan for incorporating more fun into your life (see Activity 14 in GLYLOS)
Create a social circle
Find a confidante

Daily self-care might be something simple like making time to phone a friend, buying yourself a bunch of flowers, taking time out by going for a walk or scheduling that overdue doctor's appointment that you've been putting off. It might be more elaborate, such as having a night out with friends (and <u>not</u> talking about your Loved One's problematic behavior), learning a new skill, having a weekend away or going on a picnic or to the beach.

Benefits of self-care

Aside from the obvious benefits of self-care, when you take care of your health, your fitness and your appearance, you send a powerful message to yourself and to others. The message you send is that "I am worthy of care and respect.". Other people will often make assumptions about your expectations for the way they treat you, by how you treat yourself. To send a better message to others, make self-care a top priority in your life.

Whatever aspect of self-care you choose to focus on first, planning ahead can be an effective strategy for keeping your self-care efforts a top priority.

"Love yourself first, and everything else falls in line.
You really have to love yourself to get anything done in this world." ~Lucille Ball

Planning Ahead for Self-Rewards

1. In the space below, list some ideas for rewards/self-nurturing activities. If you are stuck, refer to the list of ideas for enjoyable activities on the following page.

2. Choose one that you think you could achieve in the following week.

3. What do you need to do to make sure this happens?

4. What might get in the way of it happening?

© 2012 SMART Recovery® - All Rights Reserved

Enjoyable Activities Checklist

Mark an X in the box next to any of the activities you think you would enjoy doing.

Social:

☐ Visit a friend
☑ Call a friend
☑ Go out for a coffee
☐ Have a meal out
☐ Invite friends for dinner
☐ Ask for a hug
☐ Spend time with family
☐ Have a dinner party
☐ Join a social club

Recreational:

☐ Go for a walk
☑ Listen to music
☑ Read a novel
☐ Go to a movie
☐ Go for a jog
☐ Do some gardening
☐ Go swimming
☑ Play a sport
☑ Relax in a sauna or a spa
☐ Watch a sports event
☐ Take up dance classes
☐ Visit a place of interest
☐ Go to the beach, or the countryside

☐ Plan a holiday
☐ Sit in the sun and relax
☐ Go fishing
☐ Play a board game
☐ Do a crossword or other puzzle

Creative:

☑ Write a poem
☐ Paint or draw a picture
☐ Cook a meal or bake something
☐ Redecorate a room
☐ Learn a musical instrument
☐ Sew or knit

Pampering:

☐ Buy something nice for yourself
☐ Dress up in something nice
☐ Relax in a warm bath
☐ Have a massage
☐ Have a facial or a pedicure
☐ Watch a DVD
☐ Go to the hairdresser
☐ Prepare your favorite meal
☐ Take a nap

Educational:

☐ Visit the library
☑ Visit a museum/art gallery
☑ Enroll in a course
☐ Start a new hobby
☐ Read a non-fiction book
☐ Learn a foreign language

Other things you can think of?

☐ ....

☐ ....

☐ ....

☐ ....

☐ ....

☐ ....

☐ ....

☐ ....

☐ ....

© 2012 SMART Recovery® - All Rights Reserved

Section 2: Self-Care & Self-Rewards

Lifestyle Audit

Things I would like to do less of...	How I could do this less...

Things I would like to do more of...	How I could do this more...

"A balanced lifestyle is simply a state of being in which one has time and energy for obligations and pleasures, as well as time to live well and in a gratifying way. With its many nuances, balance can be a difficult concept to integrate into your life. Living a balanced existence, however, can help you attain a greater sense of happiness, health, and fulfillment." ~Madisyn Taylor

© 2012 SMART Recovery® - All Rights Reserved

Relaxation

Some obvious ways to relax include listening to quiet, pleasant music, using imagination & imagery to picture oneself in a relaxing scene, or using relaxation tapes. What follows here are some of the most well-known basics of relaxation. While these may be ideal for many, every person is different. Find and practice the relaxation process that works best for you.

The Four Basic Elements of the "Relaxation Response":

1. **A Quiet Environment**: Choose a place with as few distractions as possible.

2. **A Mental Device**: A sound, word, or phrase repeated silently or aloud to focus concentration (e.g., C-A-L-M). Gazing at an object (e.g., a candle) is also often effective.

3. **A Passive Attitude**: Acknowledge and then disregard all distracting thoughts — don't fight them — then return to your mental device. Don't rate or evaluate the quality of your relaxation while engaging in it — just do it and accept it as "good enough".

4. **A Comfortable Position**: Sit in a firm but comfortable chair or lie down on a firm surface.

How to relax:

1. Assume a comfortable position.

2. Allow your eyes to close.

3. Breathe in long, slow, full breaths through your nose and pay special attention to the sound of your breathing. As you breathe out, say the word or phrase you chose as your mental device. Continue to breathe easily, fully, and naturally.

4. Deeply relax all of your muscles. Allow your whole body to go limp like a rag doll. Any tense muscle or muscle group may be tightened, held tight for a few moments, and then released to create greater relaxation. Notice the increased relaxation and warmth following the release.

5. Continue this for 10 to 20 minutes. When you have finished, sit quietly for a few minutes before you stand up. Attend to, and enjoy, your increased sensations and relaxation.

6. Use this technique twice daily. Do not attempt to evaluate your success or expect it to work immediately. Such a radical shifting of gears will take time and continued practice. Practice twice each day and allow the feeling of deep relaxation to come to you, rather than trying to find it.

Note: This is best done before meals or at least two hours after meals since it tends to slow the digestive process. Also, it's best to practice relaxation at times other than just before going to sleep so that you learn how to relax and not just how to fall asleep.

Adopted from H. Benson, M.D., **The Relaxation Response**

Additional Resources

"*Get Your Loved One Sober*"

Chapter 4-Pick A Destination: "Priorities" (Oxygen Mask Rule)

Chapter 6-Let the Good Times Roll (Self-Rewards and Support Network)

From the SMART Toolbox

Enlightened Self-Interest *http://goo.gl/6OZf6*

Personal Bill of Rights [next page]

© 2012 SMART Recovery® - All Rights Reserved

Personal Bill of Rights

1. I have the right to ask for what I want.

2. I have the right to say no to requests or demands I can

3. I have the right to express all of my feelings, positive or neg

4. I have the right to change my mind.

5. I have the right to make mistakes and not have to be perfect.

6. I have the right to follow my own values and standards.

7. I have the right to say no to anything when I feel I am not ready, it is unsafe, or it violates my values.

8. I have the right to determine my own priorities.

9. I have the right not to be responsible for others' behavior, actions, feelings or problems.

10. I have the right to expect honesty from others.

11. I have the right to be angry at someone I love.

12. I have the right to be uniquely myself.

13. I have the right to feel scared and say "I'm afraid."

14. I have the right to say "I don't know."

15. I have the right not to give excuses or reasons for my behavior.

16. I have the right to make decisions based on my feelings.

17. I have the right to my own needs for personal space and time.

18. I have the right to be playful and frivolous.

19. I have the right to be healthier than those around me.

20. I have the right to be in a non-abusive environment.

21. I have the right to make friends and be comfortable around people.

22. I have the right to change and grow.

23. I have the right to have my needs and wants respected by others.

24. I have the right to be treated with dignity and respect.

25. I have the right to be happy.

26. I have the right to think about ME without feeling selfish.

If you carefully read through this list every day, eventually you will learn to accept that YOU are entitled to each of these rights.

© 2012 SMART Recovery® - All Rights Reserved

Inner Dialogue

Managing Feelings

The book "*Get Your Loved One Sober: Alternatives to Nagging, Pleading and Threatening*" is based on the scientifically validated CRAFT (Community Reinforcement and Family Training) model.

It provides guidance that you can use to recognize how you and your Loved One (LO) interact, and to help you change any unhelpful patterns in order to achieve healthier and happier results.

GYLOS advises Family & Friends (F&F) to remain calm, avoid losing their temper and avoid catastrophizing (or "awfulizing") situations in order to interact with their LO in a non-confrontational way.

This can be quite challenging for F&F who have developed habitual patterns of thinking and interacting with their LO that get in the way of calm and non-confrontational conversation.

In this section you will find tools that can help you to remain calm and matter-of-fact in situations where you may previously have found yourself becoming frustrated or angry. You will also find an introduction to Rational Emotive Behavior Therapy (REBT). REBT is central to many SMART Recovery concepts.

Rational EMOTIVE BEHAVIOR Therapy

Exchange Vocabulary

Upset feelings are usually caused by the way we are thinking about what is happening, not the events themselves. To change your feelings (and your behavior), try the following "Exchange Vocabulary."

This idea was given to me by a client, who related it to an exchange list for unhealthy foods. When you first try this new way of thinking, it might not feel right. The more you do it, however, the more natural these realistic beliefs will become.

I think you will like the results, but prove it for yourself by giving it a fair try.

© Robert F. Sarmiento, Ph.D. used with permission.

Word Exchange Table

Instead of thinking:	Try thinking:
Must	Prefer
Should	Choose To
Have To	Want
Can't	Choose Not To
Ought	Had Better
All	Many
Always	Often
Can't Stand	Don't Like
Awful	Highly Undesirable
Bad Person	Bad Behavior
I am a Failure	I Failed at

Statement Exchange Table

Instead of saying:	Try saying:
I have to do well.	I want to do well.
You shouldn't do that.	I prefer you not do that.
You never help me.	You rarely help me.
I can't stand my job.	I don't like my job.
You are a bad boy.	That behavior is undesirable.
I'm a loser.	I failed at this one task.
I need love.	I want love, but I don't need it.

Emotional Vocabulary Exchange: REBT does not endeavor to eliminate emotions. Quite to the contrary! Emotions are very useful and part of the human advantage --- When Appropriate!

Instead of saying:	Exchange With:
Anxious	Concerned
Depressed	Sad
Angry	Annoyed
Guilt	Remorse
Shame	Regret
Hurt	Disappointed
Jealous	Concern for my relationship

© 2012 SMART Recovery® - All Rights Reserved

Anti-Awfulizing

So how awful is "awful"?   How terrible is "terrible"?

It is helpful to put events into perspective, to *actively and forcefully* expand our focus to see life realistically.

We often say something is "awful" and get a feeling that it is more than 100% bad. But how can anything be *more than* 100%?

We say we *"I can't stand it!!!"* But yet we do!

So let's take these facts and begin to *manage* our thoughts and perspectives and, as a result, *directly manage* our feelings and behaviors as well!

We are not suggesting that you "sugar-coat", or minimize the situation. There is real distress and discomfort in this world. Recognition of this real distress is important.

What we are saying is, while recognizing the real distress in a situation, is to also, *at the same time*, recognize very *clearly* and very *factually*, *where* that situation lies in the spectrum of distress. And to recognize that we *can* stand it.

Here is the tool. To realize reality:

1. First rate your existing situation on a scale of 0% to 100% "bad".

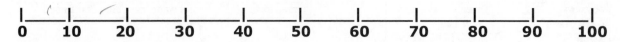

0	10	20	30	40	50	60	70	80	90	100

2. Secondly, ask yourself:

> How terrible is it?
> Could it get worse?
> Is it really as frequent as it feels?
> How long will it really last?
> *Can* I stand this?

3. Now for a bit of perspective:

> Is it as bad as a hurricane or an earthquake?
> Or say, as bad as a famine or a war?

4. And finally, for an antidote:

> Is there nothing occurring at this same time that is good?
> Is there nothing I can do to make something good happen?

It is in these simple and factual ways that we realistically manage and develop a reality-based perspective on life.

© 2012 SMART Recovery® - All Rights Reserved

Resisting Invitations to Guilt and Self-Blame

It is common for people in a close relationship with someone who has a drug and/or alcohol dependency to blame themselves and feel guilty about their Loved One's behavior. This is particularly common for parents and partners, but can also strike other family members or close friends. There can be subtle and not so subtle *invitations* to take the blame for your Loved One's (LO's) drinking or drug use, either from your LO, from those around you, or from yourself.

Sometimes these invitations are in the form of your Loved One making comments, such as "if you didn't nag me so much I wouldn't need to drink". They can also come from you, thinking thoughts such as, "if only I could be a more helpful husband (wife/mother/son), my Loved One would stop drinking".

It is normal to have regrets and wish that you could have done things differently in life. However, excessive guilt and self-blame can be a crippling force in your own life and damaging to your relationship with your Loved One. Beating yourself up about any mistakes you have made and taking on the blame for your LO's self-destructive behavior can have the following effects:

Leave you feeling stuck and helpless, unable to move forward in your own life.

Lead you to put up with behavior that is not acceptable and keep you from setting limits and standing up for your own rights. This is not helpful for you or your Loved One.

Encourage you to become overly responsible for your Loved One, thus preventing her from taking responsibility for herself.

Leave you open to being manipulated by your Loved One (which again, is not helpful to you or to her).

Leave you open to getting sick yourself. Many physical and mental health problems are associated with the stresses experienced by Family & Friends who have a LO with an addiction: burnout, depression, anxiety, heart disease, etc.

"There's no problem so awful, that you can't add some guilt to it and make it even worse." — Bill Watterson

© 2012 SMART Recovery® - All Rights Reserved

Ideas for Letting Go of Guilt and Self-Blame

- Ask yourself: "Is it really my fault?" Objectively, you cannot <u>cause</u> another person to drink or take drugs. Everyone responds to life's stressors differently and your Loved One has responded by drinking and/or taking drugs.

- Remind yourself that no one is perfect. You have probably done the best you could in the circumstances.

- Think about all the other influences on your Loved One's life that are outside of your control. These include genetics, peer group, social influences, media, etc.

- Remind yourself that you also are a product of your own set of circumstances and influences.

- Try to view yourself with compassion, rather than judgment. If you find this difficult, try thinking of yourself as your own best friend. If your friend was in your shoes, how would you respond to the situation? Would you blame your friend for their LO's addiction?

- Remind yourself that continuing to feel guilt and self-blame does not help the situation and may even be making it worse.

- If appropriate, make amends by apologizing for any hurt you might have caused in the past and talk about how things can be different in the future.

*"My Mama always said you've got to put the past behind you
before you can move on."* ~Forrest Gump

© 2012 SMART Recovery® - All Rights Reserved

Identifying "Invitations to Guilt & Self-Blame"

Can you identify any "invitations" to guilt and self-blame, either from your Loved One, from those around you, or from yourself?

How much influence has guilt and self-blame had over your relationship with your Loved One?

How could things be different if you were able to let go of feeling guilt and self-blame?

What would help you to let go of guilt and self-blame?

© 2012 SMART Recovery® - All Rights Reserved

Additional Resources

SMART Recovery Articles & Essays *http://goo.gl/LfufS*

Are You Aware of Your Thoughts?

Guilt & Resentment

Who Controls You? (see following pages)

Albert Ellis Institute: Limitless Human Emotion

"I'm at the end of my rope," "I can't take it anymore," or *"there is only so much a person can take."* These statements are entrenched in our language, in our communication, and it seems fairly futile to try to change the English language single handedly. **But are these statements helpful?** Will they give us the strength to move forward? Do these linguistic patterns allow us to express ourselves to the detriment of our ability to cope?

Full Article: *http://goo.gl/ChQvN*

© 2012 SMART Recovery® - All Rights Reserved

Who Controls You?

How Rational Emotive Behavior Therapy can help you change unwanted emotions and behaviors

By Wayne Froggatt

Most people want to be happy. They would like to feel good, avoid pain, and achieve their goals. For many, though, happiness seems to be an elusive dream. In fact, it appears that we humans are much better at disturbing and defeating ourselves! Instead of feeling good, we are more likely to worry, feel guilty and get depressed. We put ourselves down and feel shy, hurt or self-pitying. We get jealous, angry, hostile and bitter or suffer anxiety, tension and panic.

On top of feeling bad, we often act in self-destructive ways. Some strive to be perfect in everything they do. Many mess up relationships. Others worry about disapproval and let people use them as doormats. Still others compulsively gamble, smoke and overspend - or abuse alcohol, drugs and food. Some even try to end it all.

The strange thing is, most of this pain is avoidable! We don't have to do it to ourselves. Humans can, believe it or not, learn how to choose how they feel and behave.

As you think, so you feel.

People feel disturbed not by things, but by the views they take of them. Ancient words, from a first-century philosopher named Epictetus - but they are just as true now.

Events and circumstances do not cause your reactions. They result from what you tell yourself about the things that happen. Put simply, thoughts cause feelings and behaviors. Or, more precisely, events and circumstances serve to trigger thoughts, which then create reactions. These three processes are intertwined.

The past is significant. But only in so far as it leaves you with your current attitudes and beliefs. External events - whether in the past, present, or future - cannot influence the way you feel or behave until you become aware of and begin to think about them.

To fear something (or react in any other way), you have to be thinking about it. The cause is not the event - it's what you tell yourself about the event.

© 2012 SMART Recovery® - All Rights Reserved

The ABC's of feelings & behaviors

American psychologist Albert Ellis, the originator of Rational Emotive Behavior Therapy (REBT), was one of the first to systematically show how beliefs determine the way human beings feel and behave. Dr. Ellis developed the 'ABC' model to demonstrate this.

'A' refers to whatever started things off: a circumstance, event or experience - or just thinking about something which has happened. This triggers off thoughts ('B'), which in turn create a reaction - feelings and behaviors - ('C').

To see this in operation, let's meet Alan. A young man who had always tended to doubt himself, Alan imagined that other people did not like him, and that they were only friendly because they pitied him. One day, a friend passed him in the street without returning his greeting - to which Alan reacted negatively. Here is the event, Alan's beliefs, and his reaction, put into the ABC format:

A. What started things off: Friend passed me in the street without speaking to me.
B. Beliefs about A:

1. He's ignoring me. He doesn't like me.
2. I could end up without friends forever.
3. That would be terrible.
4. For me to be happy and feel worthwhile, people must like me.
5. I'm unacceptable as a friend - so I must be worthless as a person.

C. Reaction:

Feelings: worthless, depressed.
Behaviors: avoiding people generally.

Now, someone who thought differently about the same event would react in another way:

A. What started things off: Friend passed me in the street without speaking to me.

B. Beliefs about A:

1. He didn't ignore me deliberately. He may not have seen me.
2. He might have something on his mind.
3. I'd like to help if I can.

C. Reaction:

Feelings: Concerned.
Behaviors: Went to visit friend, to see how he is.

These examples show how different ways of viewing the same event can lead to different reactions. The same principle operates in reverse: when people react alike, it is because they are thinking in similar ways.

   © 2012 SMART Recovery® - All Rights Reserved

The rules we live by

What we tell ourselves in specific situations depends on the rules we hold. Everyone has a set of general 'rules'. Some will be rational, others will be self-defeating or irrational. Each person's set is different.

Mostly subconscious, these rules determine how we react to life. When an event triggers off a train of thought, what we consciously think depends on the general rules we subconsciously apply to the event.

Let us say that you hold the general rule: 'To be worthwhile, I must succeed at everything I do.' You happen to fail an examination; an event which, coupled with the underlying rule, leads you to the conclusion: 'I'm not worthwhile.'

Underlying rules are generalizations: one rule can apply to many situations. If you believe, for example: *'I can't stand discomfort and pain and must avoid them at all costs,'* you might apply this to the dentist, to work, to relationships, and to life in general.

Why be concerned about your rules? While most will be valid and helpful, some will be self-defeating. Faulty rules will lead to faulty conclusions. Take the rule: *'If I am to feel OK about myself, others must like and approve of me.'* Let us say that your boss tells you off. You may (rightly) think: 'He is angry with me' - but you may wrongly conclude: 'This proves I'm a failure.' And changing the situation (for instance, getting your boss to like you) would still leave the underlying rule untouched. It would then be there to bother you whenever some future event triggered it off.

Most self-defeating rules are a variation of one or other of the '12 Self-Defeating Beliefs' listed at the end of this article. Take a look at this list now. Which ones do you identify with? Which are the ones that guide your reactions?

What are self-defeating beliefs?

To describe a belief as self-defeating, or irrational, is to say that:

1. It distorts reality (it's a misinterpretation of what's happening); or it involves some illogical ways of evaluating yourself, others, and the world around you: awfulizing, can't-stand-it-itis, demanding and people-rating;

2. It blocks you from achieving your goals and purposes;
3. It creates extreme emotions which persist, and which distress and immobilize; and
4. It leads to behaviors that harm yourself, others, and your life in general.

Four ways to screw yourself up

There are four typical ways of thinking that will make you feel bad or behave in dysfunctional ways:

1. Awfulizing: using words like 'awful', 'terrible', 'horrible', 'catastrophic' to describe something - e.g., 'It would be terrible if …', 'It's the worst thing that could happen', 'That would be the end of the world'.

2. Cant-stand-it-itis: viewing an event or experience as unbearable - e.g., 'I can't stand it', 'It's absolutely unbearable', I'll die if I get rejected'.

3. Demanding: using 'shoulds' (moralizing) or 'musts' (musturbating) - e.g., 'I should not have done that', 'I must not fail', 'I need to be loved', 'I have to have a drink'.

4. People-rating: labeling or rating your total self (or someone else's) – e.g., 'I'm stupid /hopeless /useless /worthless.'

Rational thinking

Rational thinking presents a vivid contrast to its illogical opposite:

1. It is based on reality - it emphasizes seeing things as they really are, keeping their badness in perspective, tolerating frustration and discomfort, preferring rather than demanding, and self-acceptance;

2. It helps you achieve your goals and purposes;

3. It creates emotions you can handle; and

4. It helps you behave in ways which promote your aims and survival.

We are not talking about so-called 'positive thinking'. Rational thinking is realistic thinking. It is concerned with facts - the real world - rather than subjective opinion or wishful thinking.

Realistic thinking leads to realistic emotions. Negative feelings aren't always bad for you. Neither are all positive feelings beneficial. Feeling happy when someone you love has died, for example, may hinder you from grieving properly. Or to be unconcerned in the face of real danger could put your survival at risk. Realistic thinking avoids exaggeration of both kinds - negative and positive.

© 2012 SMART Recovery® - All Rights Reserved

The techniques of change

How does one actually set about achieving self-control and choice? The best place to start is by learning how to identify the thoughts and beliefs which cause your problems.

Next, learn how to apply this knowledge by analyzing specific episodes where you feel and behave in the ways you would like to change. It is most effective to do this in writing at first and later it will become easier to do it in your head. You connect whatever started things off, your reaction, and the thoughts which came in between. You then check out those thoughts and change the self-defeating ones. This method, called Rational Self-Analysis, uses the ABC approach described earlier, extended to include sections for setting a goal or new desired effect ('E'), disputing and changing beliefs ('D'), and, finally, further action to put those changes into practice ('F').

That final step is important. You will get there faster when you put into action what you have changed in your mind. Let us say you decide to stop feeling guilty when you do something for yourself. The next step is to do it. Spend an hour a day reading a novel. Purchase some new clothes. Have coffee with a friend or a weekend away without the family. Do the things you would previously have regarded as 'undeserved'.

Overcoming obstacles

While change is possible, it is not easy - mainly because of a very human tendency known as 'low-discomfort tolerance'.

Most of us want to be physically and emotionally comfortable. But personal change means giving up some old habits of thinking and behaving and 'safe' ways of approaching life.

Whereas before you may have blamed others for your problems, now you start to take responsibility for yourself and what you want. You risk new ways of thinking and acting. You step out into the unknown. This could increase your stress and emotional pain - temporarily. In other words, you may well feel worse before you feel better.

Telling yourself that you 'can't stand it' could lead you to avoid change. You might decide to stick with the way things are, unpleasant though it is. You know you would be better off in the long run, but you choose to avoid the extra pain now.

Or you might look for a quick solution. Do you hope that somewhere there's a fancy therapy which will cure you straight away - without you having to do anything? I meet many people who try therapist after therapist, but never stay with one approach long enough to learn anything that will help. They still live in hope, though, and often get a brief boost from meeting new therapists or therapy groups.

As well as fearing discomfort, you may also worry that you 'won't be a real person'. You think that you will end up 'pretending' to feel and behave in new ways, and imagine yourself as false or phony. Somehow, it seems, to choose how you feel seems 'less than human'.

© 2012 SMART Recovery® - All Rights Reserved

You are, though, already choosing your reactions - even though you may not be fully aware of doing so. And using conscious choice is what sets humans apart from instinct-bound animals. It is also what makes you a unique person - different to every other. So give up the notion that it is false and machine-like to use your brain to avoid bad feelings. Getting depressed, worried, and desperate does not make you more human.

You might worry that learning self-control will make you cold and unemotional, with no feelings at all. This common fear is quite misguided. The opposite is true: if you learn how to handle strong feelings you will be less afraid of them. This will free you to experience a fuller range of emotions than before.

While self-improvement may be hard, it is achievable. The blocks I have described are all self-created. They're nothing more than beliefs - ideas you can change using practical techniques you can learn.

Rational thinking is not just academic theory. People from a wide range of social and educational backgrounds have already used it successfully. You will be able to as well.

It is true that human beings start life with a biological predisposition to irrational thinking, which they then add to by learning new and harmful ways of behaving and viewing life. But there is a positive side to human nature - we also have the ability to think about our beliefs and change the dysfunctional ones.

What about problems you can't sort out on your own? Some outside help may be a useful supplement to your self-help efforts. Whether or not you have such help, though, taking responsibility for your feelings and actions will be the key to success. You will also need some hard work and perseverance. But, happily, by learning how to identify and change self-defeating beliefs and attitudes, these things can be within your control - and happiness within your reach.

© 2012 SMART Recovery® - All Rights Reserved

From Self-Defeat to Rational Living

12 Self-defeating Beliefs

1. I need love and approval from those significant to me - and I must avoid disapproval from any source.

2. To be worthwhile as a person I must achieve, succeed at whatever I do, and make no mistakes.

3. People should always do the right thing. When they behave obnoxiously, unfairly or selfishly, they must be blamed and punished.

4. Things must be the way I want them to be - otherwise life will be intolerable.

5. My unhappiness is caused by things outside my control - so there is little I can do to feel any better.

6. I must worry about things that could be dangerous, unpleasant or frightening - otherwise they might happen.

7. I can be happier by avoiding life's difficulties, unpleasantness, and responsibilities.

8. Everyone needs to depend on someone stronger than themselves.

9. Events in my past are the cause of my problems - and they continue to influence my feelings and behaviors now.

10. I should become upset when other people have problems and feel unhappy when they're sad.

11. I should not have to feel discomfort and pain – I can't stand them and must avoid them at all costs.

12. Every problem should have an ideal solution, and it is intolerable when one can't be found.

12 Rational Beliefs

1. Love and approval are good things to have, and I'll seek them when I can. But they are not necessities - I can survive (even though uncomfortably) without them.

2. I'll always seek to achieve as much as I can - but unfailing success and competence is unrealistic. Better I just accept myself as a person, separate from my performance.

3. It's unfortunate that people sometimes do bad things. But humans are not yet perfect - and upsetting myself won't change that reality.

4. There is no law which says that things have to be the way I want. It's disappointing, but I can stand it - especially if I avoid catastrophizing.

5. Many external factors are outside my control. But it is my thoughts (not the externals) which cause my feelings. And I can learn to control my thoughts.

6. Worrying about things that might go wrong won't stop them from happening. It will, though, ensure I get upset and disturbed right now!

7. Avoiding problems is only easier in the short term - putting things off can make them worse later on. It also gives me more time to worry about them!

8. Relying on someone else can lead to dependent behavior. It is OK to seek help - as long as I learn to trust myself and my own judgment.

9. The past can't influence me now. My current beliefs cause my reactions. I may have learned these beliefs in the past, but I can choose to analyze and change them in the present.

10. I can't change other people's problems and bad feelings by getting myself upset.

11. Why should I in particular not feel discomfort and pain? I don't like them, but I can stand it. Also, my life would be very restricted if I always avoided discomfort.

12. Problems usually have many possible solutions. It is better to stop waiting for the perfect one and get on with the best available. I can live with less than the ideal.

Copyright Notice:

This document is copyright © to the author (1990-97). Single copies (which include this notice) may be made for therapeutic or training purposes. For permission to use it in any other way, please contact: Wayne Froggatt, PO Box 2292, Stortford Lodge, Hastings, New Zealand. (E-mail: waynefroggatt@rational.org.nz). Comments are welcomed. This document is located on the internet site: http://www.rational.org.nz Reprinted here with permission.

The ABCs of REBT

Emotional Self-Management

Do you sometimes experience extreme upsets? Are you often frustrated, angry, sleepless, or anxious? Do you ever feel helpless or hopeless?

Emotional self-control is a valuable life-skill to possess, and it is one that is often seriously challenged in a relationship with someone who has an addiction. This section focuses on how to regain emotional self-control using the strategies and insights of Rational Emotive Behavior Therapy (REBT).

Using REBT tools, you can work to examine the role that your thoughts and beliefs play in your ability to respond to your Loved One (LO), and to other life events. You can learn to change your thoughts and beliefs in a way that can lead to improved emotional control.

REBT is a proven system designed to improve emotional self-management. Better emotional self-management empowers us. It empowers us to change those things that we can change (including our thinking). And it empowers us to accept those things that we cannot change.

What are the ABCs of REBT?

Many people consider other people or events to be the source of their distress:

Other people/Events ——▶ My Feelings/Behaviors

According to REBT (Rational Emotive Behavior Therapy), psychological distress is often experienced as a result of an individual's beliefs and perceptions. In other words, it is not people or events that directly cause us to feel and behave in certain ways, it is the *way we think* about those people and events. It is the *personal meaning* we give to an event that triggers emotions, rather than the event itself.

Consider a football game. What does a camera see? The Reds are playing against the Blues and the score is tied. In the last seconds of the game, the Reds kick a field goal, the tie is broken and the Reds win the game. Now, look at the fans: On the Red side of the stadium, the fans are cheering and appear to be happy. On the Blue side, the fans are groaning and appear to be disappointed. **One** "event" happened (field goal) and yet we see **two** *very different emotional responses*. This illustrates that it's not EVENTS that cause emotional responses. In this example, there must be something else going on to cause the fans' feelings, otherwise they would all be responding to that tie-breaking kick the same way – but they don't. What could be the reason for the different emotional responses? It is the beliefs and thoughts about the situation – how the event is being interpreted by each individual – that makes a difference in how they respond emotionally.

Other People/Events ——▶ My Beliefs/Thoughts ——▶ My Feelings/Behaviors

The ABCs of REBT help us to better manage our feelings, our emotions, and our behaviors, by investigating our beliefs and the thoughts they generate. Unhelpful beliefs can be challenged and changed.

A common situation for Family & Friends (F&F) with a Loved One (LO) who has an addiction is that the LO's behaviors (lying, overspending, legal trouble, etc.) can be challenging to those around them. F&F respond to these behaviors in many different ways. For example, it is not uncommon for F&F who have grown very frustrated to feel extreme levels of anger and/or anxiety. These feelings and the behaviors they often lead to (nagging, pleading, arguing) can become a problem of their own for the F&F.

Additionally, if the F&F have a goal of being a positive influence for a LO who has an addiction, the behaviors of nagging, pleading and arguing have been found to be counter-productive.

Using the ABCs of REBT can be an effective way of managing our own emotions and behaviors by changing our thoughts and beliefs. In doing so, we gain a calmer, more compassionate state of mind and are then better able to change our responses to our LO's challenging behaviors

© 2012 SMART Recovery® - All Rights Reserved

The ABC Model – How Thinking Affects Behavior

The ABC Model

A = The Activating event
B = Our Beliefs/perceptions about the event
C = Consequences - our feelings or behaviors

It is easy to be unaware of **B** (Beliefs/perceptions) and think that an **A** (Activating event) simply leads automatically to **C** (Consequences).   (E.g., "This situation *makes me* so angry!")

However, there is always a thought or a **B** (**B**elief) that precedes a response. It is the thought or belief that leads to the **C** (**C**onsequences), not the **A** (**A**ctivating Event) itself.

Example: Consider how Person A and Person B experience different reactions and consequences as a result of the same activating event:

Person A:

A = Getting stuck in a traffic jam on the way home or going out to dinner. *(Activating event)*

B = "This is terrible! I can't stand traffic jams!! I'm going to be late and that's unforgivable!!!" *(Beliefs/perceptions)*

C = Become stressed, arrive in a bad mood. End up having an argument. *(Consequences)*

Person B:

A = Getting stuck in a traffic jam on the way home or going out to dinner. *(Activating event)*

B = "The traffic is out of my control. There's no point getting stressed. I'm just going to listen to some relaxing music and chill out. If I'm late it's not the end of the world." *(Beliefs/perceptions)*

C = Arrive home in a relaxed state. Calmly apologize for being late. *(Consequences)*

Being aware of your thoughts, beliefs and perceptions can help you to challenge them, thereby allowing you to reduce your psychological distress and change your habitual ways of responding to challenging situations.

       © 2012 SMART Recovery® - All Rights Reserved

ABC Tool

Consider the following two scenarios:

Scenario One

A = Daughter comes home late and obviously intoxicated. *(Activating event)*

B = "She obviously doesn't care about me or she wouldn't behave this way!" *(Beliefs/perceptions)*

C = You feel very distressed and angry. You go on the attack, accusing her of being selfish, disrespectful, messing up her life, etc. You end up having an argument. The whole household is disturbed, tensions escalate and everyone feels stressed. *(Consequences)*

Scenario Two

A = Daughter comes home late and obviously intoxicated *(Activating event)*

B = ??????????? *(Beliefs/perceptions)*

C = You calmly say to daughter: "I don't like spending time with you when you've been using. I'm happy to talk to you tomorrow when you are straight. I'm going to bed now." Then you go to bed, read, practice a relaxation technique. Tensions de-escalate. You and the household feel calmer. *(Consequences)*

In scenario two above, what *beliefs/perceptions* might lead to the less stressful consequence? Or, how could you change the beliefs/perceptions from Scenario One to lead to the consequences in Scenario Two? (brainstorm)

"Nobody can hurt me without my permission." ~Mahatma Gandhi

© 2012 SMART Recovery® - All Rights Reserved

Some Common Irrational Beliefs

With the ABC model, as we explore our beliefs (**Bs**) about a situation, it is helpful to classify them as "rational" beliefs: **rBs** or "irrational" beliefs: **iBs**. **rBs** are reality-based, realistic and helpful. **iBs** are not reality-based (do not match the reality of "what is actually there") and are not helpful. Below are some examples of some common **iBs**:

- Things should be the way I think they should be. If they aren't it is terrible.

- If I make a mistake I am a failure.

- Everyone should think well of me at all times.

- As a parent, I am 100% responsible for the way my children turn out.

- I must never feel sad or unhappy.

- Everyone will judge me negatively if they know that my son/daughter/partner/parent has a problem with drugs or alcohol.

- I've given my son/daughter/partner everything, now he owes it to me to be a good person.

- If my Loved One really loved/respected me, she wouldn't use drugs.

- Using drugs means someone is a "bad" person.

- Children should respect their parents.

- If I don't keep pointing out how bad for him his drug use is, he'll never stop.

- If I leave my Loved One or ask my Loved One to leave, she will fall apart.

- I can make someone else change their behavior.

- Drug users are "helpless victims" who have no control over their behavior.

Note: Thoughts that contain "should", "must" or "ought" are often indicators of irrational, inflexible or unhelpful beliefs. If you catch yourself thinking this way, ask yourself: "where is it written that things should, must or ought to be this way?"

© 2012 SMART Recovery® - All Rights Reserved

Challenging Unhelpful Thinking

"People are disturbed not by things, but by the view which they take of them." ~Epictetus

The first step in challenging unhelpful thoughts is simply to become aware of them. Note that we are not referring to "positive thinking" where a "negative" thought or belief is replaced by an opposite "positive" thought or belief.

Rather, it is about learning to recognize and identify unhelpful thoughts, and then challenging them in order to create more helpful thoughts.

The steps involved are:

1. Become aware of your thoughts, beliefs, perceptions ("catch" them)

2. Evaluate them – are they helpful (rB) or unhelpful (iB) (rational or irrational)?*

3. If you judge them to be unhelpful or irrational, name them to yourself as such

4. Challenge or dispute unhelpful beliefs with more helpful or rational thoughts

* Note: These are some questions that can help to evaluate an irrational belief:

• Where is holding this belief getting me? Is it helpful? Or is it self-defeating?

• Where is the evidence to support my belief? Is it consistent with reality?

• Is my belief rigid or flexible?

• What helpful belief can I use to replace this unhelpful belief?

"When you take responsibility for your own thoughts, feelings and actions, you make it almost impossible for others to manipulate you or make you feel bad." ~Jonathan von Breton

Identifying & Challenging "Beliefs"

Can you identify an unhelpful belief you hold in relation to your Loved One's drug and/or alcohol use?

By using the steps outlined on the previous page, can you challenge this belief and replace it with a more helpful belief? What is that new belief?

What changes in your behavior might you notice as a result of this new belief?

"This process may involve challenging some very old, deeply held, habitual beliefs about how you, other people and the world should be. As these beliefs are so habitual, it may take some time just to recognize them. And it takes even more time to challenge them and replace them with new beliefs that work better for you. In the long run, all this effort is well worth it!" ~Jonathan von Breton

 © 2012 SMART Recovery® - All Rights Reserved

esources

ART Articles & Essays

to REBT: *http://goo.gl/080ow*

ART Toolbox

g Unhelpful Ideas: http://goo.gl/ysVgF

Rational vs. Irrational: *http://goo.gl/BvGpG*

ABC Crash Course: *http://goo.gl/tKfIi*

Tutorial

ABC Tutorial: *http://goo.gl/G69BA*

From the SMART Suggested Reading List

"Three Minute Therapy, Change Your Thinking, Change your Life"
by Michael Edelstein, Ph.D. (Glenbridge)

NOTES

Beliefs and Disputations

Rational Emotive Behavior Therapy (REBT) attributes much of the unnecessary upset or distress that we humans experience, to the unhelpful beliefs that we have learned. You can easily make yourself miserable by allowing your self-defeating or otherwise unhelpful beliefs to go unchallenged in your life.

Recognizing your unhelpful beliefs can be difficult but the payoffs are big. Learning to recognize these unhelpful beliefs for what they are (*beliefs* that can be challenged and changed) is an important skill for emotional self-management.

In this section we explore some of the more common ways of thinking that lead to unnecessary emotional upset and distress. By learning to challenge unhelpful and self-defeating beliefs, and to replace them with more helpful concepts, you can achieve a greater level of self-awareness and a greater level of emotional self-management.

The ABC Model – How Thinking Affects Behavior

The ABC Model

A = The Activating event
B = Our Beliefs/perceptions about the event
C = Consequences - our feelings or behaviors

It is easy to be unaware of **B** (Beliefs/perceptions) and think that an **A** (Activating event) simply leads automatically to **C** (Consequences).   (E.g., "This situation *makes me* so angry!")

However, there is always a thought or a **B** (**B**elief) that precedes a response. It is the thought or belief that leads to the **C** (**C**onsequences), not the **A** (**A**ctivating Event) itself.

Example: Consider how Person A and Person B experience different reactions and consequences as a result of the same activating event:

Person A:

A = Getting stuck in a traffic jam on the way home or going out to dinner. ***(Activating event)***

B = "This is terrible! I can't stand traffic jams!! I'm going to be late and that's unforgivable!!!" ***(Beliefs/perceptions)***

C = Become stressed, arrive in a bad mood. End up having an argument. ***(Consequences)***

Person B:

A = Getting stuck in a traffic jam on the way home or going out to dinner. ***(Activating event)***

B = "The traffic is out of my control. There's no point getting stressed. I'm just going to listen to some relaxing music and chill out. If I'm late it's not the end of the world." ***(Beliefs/perceptions)***

C = Arrive home in a relaxed state. Calmly apologize for being late. ***(Consequences)***

Being aware of your thoughts, beliefs and perceptions can help you to challenge them, thereby allowing you to reduce your psychological distress and change your habitual ways of responding to challenging situations.

© 2012 SMART Recovery® - All Rights Reserved

A Closer Look at Beliefs (the "B" in the ABC Model)

When doing the ABCs, it can help to know that most irrational (unhelpful, self-sabotaging) beliefs fall into one of three categories.

(1) Beliefs about yourself. For instance: *"I must do well — or else I'm no good;"*

(2) Beliefs about others. For instance: *"Others must treat me nicely and kindly and just the way I want — or else they are no good,"* and,

(3) Beliefs about life in general. For instance: *"The world must make it easy for me to get what I want and must create circumstances so that things always go my way — or else it's a lousy, rotten world."*

These kinds of beliefs create the three main emotional upsets of

(1) anxiety/guilt/shame,
(2) anger/hostility/rage, and
(3) depression.

They also create demandingness, whining, condemnation and damnation of ourselves and others, and exaggeration beyond the bounds of reality.

Unpleasant emotions are unavoidable, and can even be motivating and helpful. But we humans have the natural ability to escalate unpleasant feelings to the level of emotional upset, which easily defeats us. In REBT, we are not trying to eliminate all unpleasant emotions, just those that hinder us. Disputing allows us to eliminate irrational (unhelpful, self-sabotaging) thinking that contributes to our disturbed emotions. Then we may remain "reasonably" sad or concerned, so that we can be more effective at dealing with difficult situations.

To accomplish this we:

D. Dispute the irrational "Bs". Learn to recognize the inaccurate beliefs and distortions of reality which we use to defeat ourselves and needlessly make ourselves miserable.

E. Exchange effective, more accurate, rational self-statements for our dysfunctional beliefs.

Don't believe everything you think!

© 2012 SMART Recovery® - All Rights Reserved

The Notorious Five Ways We Upset Ourselves

Irrational Beliefs (iBs): How do we find the iB (the unhelpful belief) that is prompting us to feel upset? Many times, the answer lies in the **Notorious Five:**

<u>Demanding</u> (shoulds, musts)
Often we can ask ourselves "what's the demand here?" and find an answer to our iB investigation. For example, the demand might be "My LO MUST stop using" or "I CAN'T STAND this anymore!"

> **The Three Major Musts of REBT**
>
> There are Three Basic Irrational Demands that we make:
>
> 1. I must be perfect in everything I do and be loved by everyone important to me or I am a failure/unlovable.
>
> 2. Others must treat me with respect and consideration at all times, and otherwise act as I think they should, or they are damnable people.
>
> 3. The world must give me what I want, nothing I don't, and be easily enjoyable and hassle-free — or my life is terrible.

<u>Overgeneralizing</u> (absolutes)
"This ALWAYS happens to me" or "I NEVER get a break" are a couple of examples of "absolutes" we can use to fuel an upset. Absolutes such as these are unrealistic and offer us nothing but a basis for an undesirable emotional/behavioral outcome.

<u>Awfulizing</u> (it's terrible, horrible)
Magnifying how bad the situation is by describing it in such terms as "terrible, awful or horrible" often isn't consistent with reality.

<u>Rating/Blaming</u> (judging, label attachment)
Harshly judging and labeling makes it difficult to see that it's likely a *behavior* we are trying to describe, and not really *a person*... whether it be us or someone else.

<u>Low Frustration Tolerance</u> **(LFT)**
Typically this manifests itself as "I can't stand it!" The fact is we CAN stand it, we are simply upsetting ourselves through our own Low Frustration Tolerance. If we TRULY couldn't stand it, we'd pass out, die, or explode.

Harmful irrational beliefs cloud our consciousness with distortions, misconceptions, overgeneralizations, and oversimplifications. They limit and narrow our outlook, making it difficult to sort out problems and make decisions.

While not *all* iBs can be found in these five areas, *most* of them can. Once we have tracked down our iB (or iBs), we can move on to the process of Disputation.

© 2012 SMART Recovery® - All Rights Reserved

Unhelpful Thinking Patterns

Below are examples of some common unhelpful statements. Which of the Notorious Five is behind each? **D**emandingness? **O**vergeneralization? **R**ating & Blaming? **A**wfulizing? **L**ow Frustration Tolerance?

_____Things should be the way I think they should be or it is terrible.

_____If I make a mistake I am a failure.

_____Everyone should think well of me at all times.

_____As a parent, I am 100% responsible for the way my children turn out.

_____I must never feel sad or unhappy.

_____Everyone will judge me negatively if they know that my Loved One has a problem with drugs or alcohol.

_____I've given my Loved One everything, now he owes it to me to be a good person.

_____If my Loved One really loved /respected me she wouldn't use drugs.

_____Using drugs means someone is a "bad" person.

_____Children should respect their parents.

_____If I don't keep pointing out how bad for him his drug use is, he'll never stop.

_____If I leave my Loved One or ask my Loved One to leave, she will fall apart.

_____No matter what I try, nothing changes. This is driving me crazy!!!!

_____Drug users are "helpless victims" who have no control over their behavior.

"There is nothing either good or bad, but thinking makes it so." ~Shakespeare

---

 © 2012 SMART Recovery® - All Rights Reserved

Disputations

We can challenge our beliefs using disputing questions to ascertain their validity in our life. Disputing is done in the form of asking questions about the Belief (B). We can dispute our beliefs using facts, logic and practical considerations.

Scientific/Evidence-Based

Here's where we examine the objective reality of a situation. Some evidence-based disputations include:

> Where's the evidence that supports this belief?
> Do I have proof of this?
> Even if this is true, is it possible for me not to upset myself over it?
> What would I lose of value if I didn't continue to believe this?

Logical

This type of disputation is used to investigate the logic of the belief, to see if the belief is consistent with valid reasoning. As an example, if I believe I'm a failure because I have failed at a particular task, I can ask myself if this follows good logic: is it valid to conclude that the event (of failure) makes ME a failure? Some disputations using the Logical method are:

> Does it follow that if X happens, that Y is true?
> Could I be over-generalizing?
> How do I know this is a fact?
> What's wrong with the notion here that I'm so special that this only applies to me?
> Why must this be so?

Practical/Functional/Pragmatic

A practical disputation addresses the emotional/behavioral reaction itself. This is like putting your reaction into a CBA and investigating the costs and benefits of holding your belief. In fact, doing a CBA on a long-held belief that is causing you problems is a detailed type of practical disputation.

Some common Practical disputations include:

> Will my belief help me to resolve this issue?
> Does this belief help me to reach my goal?
> Why hold on to a belief that causes me so much trouble?
> Is it possible for me to think differently about this?

One thing all these have in common is the basic question: Can I PROVE this belief to be rational?

Once we have challenged the old beliefs and found them to be unhelpful, we can then move on to forming a New Effective Belief (E), decide how we can functionally apply it (F), using our Goals (G) as a guideline.

Asking Disputing Questions

Below are some examples of common unhelpful statements. In the space below, challenge these statements using disputing questions as suggested on the previous page. Are these beliefs rational (helpful)? If not, what new effective belief might you want to substitute?

As a parent, I am 100% responsible for the way my children turn out.

If my Loved One really loved/respected me she wouldn't use drugs.

If I don't keep pointing out how bad for him his drug use is, he'll never stop.

© 2012 SMART Recovery® - All Rights Reserved

Additional Resources

From the SMART Articles & Essays

Introduction to REBT: *http://goo.gl/080ow*

From the SMART Toolbox

Challenging Unhelpful Ideas: *http://goo.gl/ysVgF*

Rational vs. Irrational: *http://goo.gl/BvGpG*

ABC Crash Course: *http://goo.gl/tKfIi*

Tutorial

ABC Tutorial: *http://goo.gl/G69BA*

From the SMART Suggested Reading List

"Three Minute Therapy, Change Your Thinking, Change your Life"
by Michael Edelstein, Ph.D. (Glenbridge)

© 2012 SMART Recovery® - All Rights Reserved

NOTES

Positive Communication

Are you having problems talking to your Loved One (LO) in a way that is nurturing and beneficial to you both?

When relationships are troubled, and many relationships where addiction is involved *are* troubled, there are some predictable ways that communication styles deteriorate. These changes happen in all areas of communication, not just in our communication about the addiction.

Typically, in troubled relationships, both parties begin to favor negative comments, rather than positive comments. They converse in terms of "you" statements rather than "I" statements and they tend to disregard each other's point of view. Finally, both parties stop sharing responsibility for the situation and begin blaming each other. These ineffective communication styles can be changed.

The book *Get Your Loved One Sober* (GYLOS) is about changing the relationship with your LO and communication is a key to doing that.

Learning to communicate in a positive way — and learning to listen to your LO in an effective way — are skills that can lead to an improved relationship and the possibility of collaboration vs. confrontation.

Communication Styles

Generally speaking, communication can be characterized by four different styles. Which one do you most frequently use to deal with conflicts in your relationships?

1. Passive communication

- Not standing up for your rights

- Not setting limits or boundaries on another's behavior

- Continually putting other's needs before your own

- Taking on the role of "martyr"

- Not being able to say "no"

2. Aggressive Communication

- Bullying and intimidating others to get what you want

- Threatening people

- Ignoring the needs and rights of others

- Shouting, yelling, screaming or physically abusing others

3. Passive-Aggressive Communication

- Indirectly communicating – e.g., slamming doors; giving the "silent treatment"; saying something that is designed for your Loved One to hear without saying it to her directly

- Using sarcasm/put downs

- Using humor to be nasty or hurtful

4. Assertive Communication

- Being direct and honest

- Being able to negotiate – having a sense of give and take

- Asking for your own needs to be met, while respecting the needs of others

- Being able to say "no" and set limits

- Being able to acknowledge when you are in the wrong

Positive Communication

Four important areas of interpersonal communication are often abandoned when relationships run into hard times. Both parties tend to stop using statements that are *Positive*, begin with *"I"*, express *Understanding*, and demonstrate a willingness to *Share* responsibility for the situation. The acronym **PIUS** can be used to help remember how to get our communication back on track.

Be **POSITIVE**. Include positive comments in your conversation (and avoid negative comments). This not only helps the listener, but also helps you remember that you do appreciate something about the other person. Think of something that you really like about them or just tell them you love them. Become conscious of those things that you tend to communicate in a negative way and reframe them using positive phrasing. (I.e., say what you want, not what you don't want)

Use **"I" statements**. The "I" statement is one of the best communication tools that we have. It helps us to speak to another person in a way that communicates our needs or wishes without blaming or criticizing the other person. When others feel blamed or criticized, they usually become defensive. (see Exercise - *I* Statements)

> *"I feel."* When you communicate your feelings you have a choice. Blaming your Loved One (e.g., "You make me so mad." "You always make me sad.") will put your LO on the defensive. Accept responsibility for your feelings when communicating with your LO. (E.g., "When you drink, *I feel* sad and worried".)

> *"I want."* Let your LO know what you would like from him in place of a current behavior. Make your request reasonable and something your LO can actually do. (E.g., *"I would like it* if you could call me if you will be late for dinner." *"I would like it* if we could spend time together going to the movies or out to eat.")

Be **UNDERSTANDING**. Show your LO that you care about her and respect her enough to try to understand her point of view (even if you do not agree with it). LISTEN to her. Really listen. Ask questions; reflect back what you hear in a non-judgmental tone. Understanding your LO's point of view will make it easier for you to find some common ground. When you show that you are trying to understand something about another person, they are more likely to accept that *you* have something important to share with them.

Accept and **SHARE** responsibility. Neither one of you is perfect. Understanding and acknowledging your part in the problem goes a long way in breaking out of the pattern of conflict.

> *"The way you talk to your loved one not only reflects how you feel about him,*
> *but also sets the tone for his reactions to you."* ~GYLOS

© 2012 SMART Recovery® - All Rights Reserved

"I" Statements

Blaming/Negative Statement	Positive "I" Statement
You and your buddies made a mess of this place.	Ex: I'm glad your friends like coming here. Could you help me keep it tidy so it looks good for company?
You're no fun to be with when you've been drinking.	
Don't yell at the kids like that!	
I can't stand it when you lie to me.	
You missed my parent's anniversary party on purpose!	
What's wrong with you?! Why don't you get a job!	
You never listen to me when I'm talking to you.	
How could you do this? You took money out of my purse without asking!	
If I'm going to go to the trouble of cooking for you, the least you could do is show up on time.	
You're an accident waiting to happen when you're drinking (or using).	
You're a disgusting slob.	
What are you thinking, using drugs in front of the kids????	

© 2012 SMART Recovery® - All Rights Reserved

Section 6: Positive Communication

Communication Tips

1. Plan Ahead. Think about what you want to say and how you are going to say it.

2. Choose the right time; that is, when you both have time, are feeling calm and it is likely that your Loved One can be receptive.   Note: It's best to avoid communicating something important to someone who is intoxicated; in those situations, keep conversation to a minimum.

3. Be brief and stick to the subject. Your Loved One will be more likely to stay in the conversation. Bringing up old situations and disagreements is likely to result in your LO becoming defensive about the past.

4. Be specific. Target specific behaviors rather than making generalizations Generalizations are likely to make your Loved One feel blamed and judged. .(E.g., "It seems like you get drunk every weekend.")

5. Maintain a calm tone of voice.

6. Be **POSITIVE**.

7. Use **"I" Statements.**

8. Be **UNDERSTANDING.**

9. Accept and **SHARE** responsibility.

"There is no point in trying to have a rational conversation with someone who's brain is under the influence of a drug." ~GYLOS

© 2012 SMART Recovery® - All Rights Reserved

Planning a Conversation Using PIUS

What *specific behavior* do I want to address?

When would be a good time(s) for this conversation?

Positive statements

I statements

Understanding (listen, ask questions, reflect back what you hear)

Accept and share responsibility

End with a Positive statement

© 2012 SMART Recovery® - All Rights Reserved   Section 6: Positive Communication

Listening

When you are communicating with someone who is rigidly holding on to their point of view, you gain nothing by disagreeing. More importantly, when you disagree and try to force the other person to accept your point of view, the other person often shuts down.

Listen in Order to Disarm

Although we hear their words, quite often we *aren't really listening* to our LO. Instead we are busy with reacting, judging, providing solutions, and disagreeing.

Effective listening requires two things. First, we must gain a clear understanding of our LO's point of view. Second, we must convey that understanding back to our LO.

Listening with genuine concern and respect, using open-ended questions and reflective listening, is the key to opening the way for our LO to care about *our opinion,* so that we can find ways to partner together to solve problems.

Empathize In Order to Befriend

When we can master the skills of non-judgmental listening, our LO feels understood, respected and more trusting. When we can demonstrate that we understand his/her point of view and how he feels about his situation, there is nothing to argue about and our LO becomes less defensive and more open to hearing our perspective.

So, the first step is to *stop arguing* and *start listening* to your Loved One in a way that leaves him feeling that his point of view — including his rationale for any addictive behaviors — is being respected.

You don't have to agree with his reality — the realness of his experience — but you do need to listen to it and genuinely respect it.

To do this you will have to drop your agenda. Listen with only one goal: to empathize with your Loved One's point of view and reflect your understanding back to him.

When you feel empathy and convey it, your Loved One will very likely feel understood and respected. Whenever you convey that you understand how your Loved One is feeling, his or her defensiveness will decrease and his or her openness to *your opinion* will increase.

The best listening skill is to be non-judgmental. When you judge someone when they're talking, the other person often shuts down. Non-judgmental listening gives the other person a sense of freedom and acceptance.

© 2012 SMART Recovery® - All Rights Reserved

Open-Ended Questions

Asking open-ended questions invites elaboration and thinking more deeply about an issue. It is a helpful skilll for gaining insight into your Loved One's point of view.

Open-ended questions cannot be answered with a single word (yes/no) or short phrase.

Examples of Open and Closed Questions

       Would you like pasta for dinner?   Closed

       Won't you tell me about your trip? . . . Open

Change the following questions from close-ended to open-ended questions:

Closed Question: "So you didn't like that, huh?"

    Your open-ended version: _____

Closed Question: "Nice weather we're having, isn't it?"

    Your open-ended version: _____

Closed Question: "Did you have a good day?"

    Your open-ended version: _____

Closed Question: "Are you tired?"

    Your open-ended version: _____

Closed Question: "Don't you think it would be better if you did your homework, first?"

    Your open-ended version: _____

Reflective Listening

Reflective Listening turns down the volume on everyone's anger, builds trust, and mends fences. The reason is that you listen with only one goal: to understand the other person's point of view and reflect your understanding back to him. You don't comment on what he just said, you don't point out ways in which you think he's wrong, you don't judge, or react in any way. It sounds easy but it is a skill that doesn't come naturally to most people. To succeed, you will need to learn to *really listen and not react* to what your loved one feels, wants, and believes. Then, after you think you understand what you were told, you will need to reflect back, in your own words, your understanding of what you just heard. The trick is to do this without commenting, disagreeing, or arguing.

Exercise: Thinking Reflectively

In this exercise, assume the role of the "curious listener". Respond to the speaker's statement with as many questions as you can, using the format: "Do you mean that _____?"

Example:

> **Speaker:** One thing I like about myself is that I'm organized.
> **Listener:** Do you mean that you keep your desk tidy?
> **S:** No!
> **L:** Do you mean that you manage your time well?
> **S:** Yes.
> **L:** Do you mean that you always know where to find things?
> **S:** No.

Speaker: If a relative of mine had permission to brag about me, she would say that I'm good with my hands.

Listener: Respond to the speaker by asking: "Do you mean you _____?"
Try to come up with at least 5 closed questions.

© 2012 SMART Recovery® - All Rights Reserved

Exercise: Forming Reflections

This exercise develops your skill in making "Reflective Statements"

The questions asked in the last exercise are very close to reflective listening, but not quite. *The process* of generating reflective statements is the same as in the prior exercise: The listener makes a guess about the speaker's meaning and offers this to the speaker for response. This involves reflecting back what was said *along with t*he listener's best guess at the speaker's feelings about what was said. With reflective statements the listener reflects back to the speaker using statements rather than questions.

In this exercise the listener (you) will offer a hypothesis about what the speaker means. This hypothesis is in the form of a *statement* rather than a *question* (difference in inflection at the end of the sentence). A good reflective listening response is a *statement.* Its inflection turns *down* at the end.

 Example:

> "You're angry about what I said?" (up)

> vs. "You're angry about what I said. (down)

It may feel strange to make a statement instead of asking a question; for example it may feel presumptuous, as if you are "telling the person what she feels". Yet statements usually work better in conveying understanding and empathy.

You may find it helpful to have some words to get you started in making reflective listening statements. The common element is the word "you."

Examples:

> So you feel...

> It sounds like you...

> You're wondering if...

> You...

Using the suggested starter phrases above, practice your reflective listening skills in the following scenarios.

1. Speaker says: "One thing I like about myself is that I am a good judge of character."

   Listener: Write at least three reflective statements below and then practice saying them aloud as a statement (inflection turned down at the end).

2. Speaker says: "One thing you should know about me is that I like to party!"

   Listener: Write at least three reflective statements below and then practice saying them aloud as a statement (inflection turned down at the end).

3. Speaker says: "One thing I would like to change about myself is my tendency to run out of money before the week is out."

   Listener: Write at least three reflective statements below and then practice saying them aloud as a statement (inflection turned down at the end).

© 2012 SMART Recovery® - All Rights Reserved

Additional Resources

Compassionate Attitude

To reinforce a compassionate attitude, with your attention geared to the other person, tell yourself:

1. Step 1: "Just like me, this person is seeking happiness in his/her life."
2. Step 2: "Just like me, this person is trying to avoid suffering in his/her life."
3. Step 3: "Just like me, this person has known sadness, loneliness and despair."
4. Step 4: "Just like me, this person is seeking to fill his/her needs."
5. Step 5: "Just like me, this person is learning about life."

From the book: "*I'm Right, You're Wrong, Now What?*" (leapinstitute.org)

"If the person you are arguing with accuses you of not listening or not understanding them, *they're right.*" Reflective listening and empathy are key for the other person to "feel heard".

"You will not win based on the strength of your argument, but on the strength of your relationship." ~Xavier Amador, author "*I'm Right, You're Wrong, Now What?*"

NOTES

Healthy Boundaries Part I

Identifying and Communicating Your Boundaries

Boundaries are the guidelines that we identify to define what we feel are reasonable, safe and permissible ways for other people to behave around us and to treat us. Initially, it may be easy to shy away from the topic of boundaries, especially if we think of boundaries as restrictive walls that close us in and shut others out. A more helpful way to think of boundaries is to think about the true function they serve: clear boundaries can minimize miscommunication and free us to enjoy a healthier relationship with our Loved One (LO).

Addictive behaviors are often in direct conflict with healthy boundaries. In active addiction, respectful behavior that you used to take for granted is often replaced by new unacceptable behaviors. Learn to leverage the communication skills in the previous section to effectively communicate with your LO about your feelings and expectations regarding these new behaviors. Restoring healthy boundaries is a key to re-establishing mutual respect in your interactions with your LO.

Healthy Boundaries

Why are Boundaries relevant for Family & Friends?

All people in healthy relationships have healthy boundaries running smoothly in the background as the basis for mutual respect between the two parties. We may never think about them — UNTIL the relationship becomes unhealthy or experiences problems.

Without healthy boundaries, when facing challenging relationship issues such as those that often accompany addiction, it's common to give up or change our own values in order to keep the peace and hold onto the relationship. Healthy boundaries, on the other hand, can allow us to *maintain and enjoy the relationship more* while at the same time staying true to our own values and our own direction. People with addiction and those who are close to them are often found to have weak boundaries and can benefit from personal work to explore, define and communicate their personal boundaries.

What do we mean by "Boundaries"?

Boundaries are:

> **Boundaries are guidelines, rules, or limits** that we identify *for ourselves* about what *we desire* in the way of reasonable, safe and permissible ways for other people to behave around us. E.g., "I do not want to be subjected to second hand smoke." " I do expect you to pay your share of the rent by the first of the month."
>
> Boundaries also include those decisions we make about how we will respond when someone steps outside those limits we have identified.

Boundaries are not:

> **Boundaries are not brick walls.** Walls are meant to *keep people out*. Boundaries are more like fences, meant to *mark out personal space, rights, and preferences*. It is difficult or impossible to have a relationship with someone on the other side of a brick wall. It is easier and very possible to have a healthy relationship with someone on the other side of a gated fence.
>
> **Healthy boundaries are not "about the other"** person or their actions. They are **"about the self"**. Having healthy boundaries is how we remind ourselves and others that our trust, affection, time, energy, health and friendship have value and will be protected. Healthy boundaries are a sign of respect for ourselves and our desires. E.g., "I do not want to be subjected to second hand smoke, please smoke outside." "I understand that you have had a lot of unexpected expenses this month. Please remember that the rent is due on the first."

What sort of person has Boundaries?

All people have a sense of how they wish to be treated, so all people do have boundaries even if they don't use that term. People who are not well practiced in communicating their boundaries frequently experience enormous frustration when others violate their rules of acceptable behavior (boundaries). Learning to effectively communicate our healthy boundaries can work to alleviate this frustration.

Boundary Questionnaire

True or False:

___ I loan money to my Loved One (LO), but often do not get repaid. *

___ I am supporting someone financially who should be able to support him/herself. *

___ My LO lies to me, covers up the truth of his/her activities. *

___ I fail to speak up when I am being treated poorly. *

___ I frequently agree to do things in order to keep the peace, or to please others. *

___ My LO has been responsible for causing damage or theft of my property. *

___ I give and give and give in this relationship — and in return, I get less and less and less. *

___ I don't give any thought to my own happiness.**

___ My LO sometimes disappears for long periods of time without making contact. *

___ I frequently feel angry in response to my LO's behaviors. *

___ I feel like I can't make plans, because my LO is so unpredictable. *

___ My LO puts lives at risk by driving while under the influence. *

___ I can *only* be happy if my LO is doing well. Otherwise I'm anxious.**

___ My LO is emotionally unavailable much or all of the time.*

___ My LO does not accept responsibility for any household chores. *

___ I don't feel like I'm thriving, only surviving.**

___ My LO is verbally or physically abusive. *

___ My LO expects me to be a backup alarm for work/school if he/she oversleeps. *

___ My LO doesn't clean up after him/herself. *

___ My LO does not follow through on promises. *

* Your boundaries *may be* being crossed by another
 ** You *may be* crossing your *own* boundaries

  © 2012 SMART Recovery® - All Rights Reserved

Indentifying & Communicating Boundaries

How do we know we have a boundary issue that needs addressing?

Some signs that we may need to focus on boundaries:

> **Feelings of:** depression, fatigue, anxiety, burnout, powerlessness, panic and extreme anger

> **Attempting to:** keep the peace by putting up with things, trying to control things we cannot control

> **Problems with:** making decisions, defining goals for ourselves, getting things done (because we've devoted ourselves to trying to manage someone else's life), addictions of our own

Who benefits from boundary communication?

One of the consequences of addiction is a Loved One's (LO's) behavior that is often *unknowingly* hurtful, disrespectful, or disturbing to Family & Friends (F&F).

In the short-term it may seem easier to keep the peace and not add to the drama by discussing your Loved One's disturbing behavior.

But think about the long-term: What is the likelihood that things will improve if F&F never share with their LO how their behavior is affecting those closest to them? What is the likely long-term effect on F&F if they never speak up? Is it possible that your LO might mistake your patience and tolerance for acceptance of their behaviors?

Healthy boundaries provide a way for F&F to respectfully communicate the problems they are experiencing with their LO's behavior and to request alternate behaviors.

> *"YOU are at the center of everything. YOU are the most important player.*
> *You need to have the energy and heart to keep going.*
> *To make sure you do, you absolutely must take care of yourself."* ~GYLOS

How to establish healthy boundaries:

In order to establish healthy boundaries between yourself and others:

First: Identify the symptoms of your boundaries currently being or having been violated or ignored. Some symptoms to look for: *anger, frustration, feeling powerless or hopeless*

Second: Take responsibility for *your own upsets* — Identify the irrational or unhealthy thinking and beliefs that have led you to allow your boundaries to be ignored or violated. The ABC Tool (Section 4) is an excellent resource for this.

Third: Identify new, more rational, healthy thinking and beliefs which will encourage you to change your behaviors so that you build healthy boundaries between yourself and others.

Fourth: Identify new communication skills you will need in order to sustain healthy boundaries between you and others going forward. The key word here is "sustain".

Fifth: Implement your new healthy boundary-building beliefs and behaviors in your life so that your *space*, *privacy* and *rights* are no longer ignored or violated.

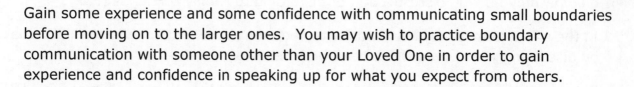

Where to start:

Gain some experience and some confidence with communicating small boundaries before moving on to the larger ones. You may wish to practice boundary communication with someone other than your Loved One in order to gain experience and confidence in speaking up for what you expect from others.

Whether you start with others or with your LO, consider beginning by addressing smaller issues (such as not being inconvenienced by a co-worker; your LO not cleaning up after herself; your LO not participating in household chores) before tackling larger and more personal issues such as behaviors directly related to substance abuse.

What are some examples of boundary problems that you might like to address?

© 2012 SMART Recovery® - All Rights Reserved

How to communicate a boundary effectively

Communicating in a direct and honest manner is a critical component to setting boundaries. It is impossible to have a healthy relationship with someone who has no boundaries, and who cannot communicate honestly and directly. Learning how to set boundaries is a necessary step in learning to be a friend to ourselves and others.

Since boundaries are "about the self" and not "about the other", they are best communicated in the form of "I" statements:

Sample format for communicating boundaries:

> **Inform:** When you do: (*YOUR BEHAVIOR*) I feel: (*MY REACTION*)
> **Request:** Can I ask you to (*STOP or CHANGE this BEHAVIOR*)?

> **Example**: When you *have the TV turned up loud* I feel *frustrated* because I can't hear the baby monitor. Can I ask you to turn down the volume, please?

> **Example:** When you *don't let me know where you are*, I feel very *worried* about you. I would like it in the future if you could *call and tell me you are going to be late.*

What to expect when you communicate a boundary

No matter how skillfully F&F communicate a boundary, LOs may likely see the boundary as an attempt to control their behavior and, if this is the case, resistance is to be expected. *Reminder:* In the event of a hostile response from a LO, your immediate safety is the first priority. Postponing boundary communication may be the best option.

The boundary communication may need to be redelivered, in a calm manner, multiple times, over several days, using the "I" statement format or using a PIUS style of communication. (*see Section 6: Positive Communication*) Reminder: Boundaries communicated to a LO who is intoxicated may not be "heard".

If your LO continues to cross the boundary, a further step, in the form of deciding and communicating what action you will take in response to future violations, may be required (see Section 11: Healthy Boundaries, Part II).

Healthy Boundaries Summary

Basic Guiding Principles For Boundaries

—Boundaries are invisible fences, essential to protect me

—It is my responsibility to know, communicate, and protect my boundaries and limits

—When I know my own boundaries, I can respect others' boundaries

Facts Regarding Boundaries

—*No one* has or keeps perfect boundaries

—*Everyone* struggles to establish and maintain healthy boundaries throughout life

—Boundaries offer protection from others who might knowingly or unknowingly control us, hurt us, abuse us, manipulate us, or use us

(Source: Michigan Reachout)

The Importance of Boundaries When Dealing With Addiction

We all have personal boundaries, and when we are in healthy, functional relationships, "boundary violations" are often effortlessly worked out between the people involved.

Consider that, as a friend or family member of someone with addiction, we are often affected by a Loved One's maladaptive behaviors. We may find ourselves feeling angry, frustrated, disrespected or powerless. These are signs that personal boundaries are being violated — yours *and your Loved One's*. Communicating and working on "boundary violations" requires effort and the communication is often challenging — but not impossible, and definitely worth the effort.

When my boundaries are violated, there are several things I can do:

I can do an ABC (see Section 4: The ABCs of REBT). I can choose to accept that this person's behaviors "are what they are" and I can become less upset as a result of dropping my demand that they be something they are not. I will still be hurt and possibly still angry but hopefully calmer, and able to express my feelings in a non-confrontational way.

I can communicate to my Loved One about how their behaviors are affecting me.

I can request that the behaviors be changed.

I can decide upon, and communicate, my plan for dealing with future hurtful behaviors if my request is not honored (see Section 11: Healthy Boundaries, Part II).

I can follow through with my plan to protect my boundaries (see Section 11: Healthy Boundaries, Part II).

By taking action and following through with my plan to protect my own personal boundaries with a Loved One who has an addiction, I not only preserve my own sense of self-worth, but my Loved One experiences natural consequences of his/her behaviors. By <u>not protecting</u> my own boundaries, my Loved One gets the message that his/her behaviors are acceptable.

 © 2012 SMART Recovery® - All Rights Reserved

Hula Hoop Boundary Analogy

Remember the hula hoop? Imagine that you have one around you right now. It magically hovers around your waist area all the time. Now imagine that everyone else has one around them, too.

So often, we spend an incredible amount of time and energy on things that we can't control. And then we get mad at ourselves for failing to do what was never possible to do in the first place because it was not within our control.

Ok, you might say, but what has that got to do with a hula hoop? Think of the hula hoop as your very own sorting tool for differentiating between what you can and cannot control. In other words, if it is *in* your hula hoop, you can probably control it. If it is *out* of your hula hoop, you cannot control it and all efforts to do so are wasted.

What is IN your hula hoop?

- Your body
- Your thoughts
- Your actions
- Your opinions
- Your values
- Your dreams
- Your wishes

What is OUT of your hula hoop?

- EVERYTHING ELSE!
- other people
- other people's thoughts
- other people's actions
- the weather
- etc, etc, etc

Are you starting to get the picture here? What is YOURS is in your hula hoop and those are really the only things you can control. Everything that is not yours belongs outside the hula hoop.

Now, this may sound pretty simple. But you would be amazed when you really start doing some sorting, how often you find yourself in someone else's hula hoop. Imagine that for a minute. Picture yourself merrily hula-ing away with your own hoop. Then picture yourself hula-ing two hoops - ahh!! you may say, "I can hula two hoops" and you may be right. But can you hula two hoops WITH ANOTHER PERSON IN ONE OF THEM? Hmm? Can you ?

NOTES

Safety and Support

It is common for substance abuse and violence to go hand-in-hand. Violence includes verbal, psychological and physical abuse.

Whether or not you are currently experiencing any of the forms of violence identified in this section, recognize the potential for violent behavior. This section offers tools and suggestions for planning those actions you may need to take in the future to keep yourself and other family members safe.

An important part of self-care and safety is working to develop a support network for yourself. Many times, people who have a Loved One with an addiction come to realize that they have become isolated from others. Out of shame or fear of judgment, they may have stopped spending time with others in their efforts to hide the reality of their situation from their friends and family.

Isolation can lead to increased stress, depression, anxiety and loss of perspective on what is "normal" or acceptable. Developing a support network is a vital aspect of "self-care".

Defining "Violence"

What is violent behavior?

"...violence is more than just hitting or pushing. It is also injury by distortion (as in twisting your words into something hateful) and profanation (swearing at you). Violence is any angry, destructive force (like throwing things) as well as vehement discordance (like threatening to shut you up for good).......Contrary to what some television shows and movies might suggest, violence is not a natural part of love or sexuality." Source: Get Your Loved One Sober

Examples of "violence":

Physical Violence

Inappropriate physical contact (e.g., hitting, choking, pushing, slapping)
Throwing objects
Locking you out of the home
Smashing, damaging, stealing or selling your possessions
Driving recklessly
Punching walls or doors

Verbal Abuse

Humiliation/insults/shaming
Yelling/swearing/screaming
Criticizing your appearance or actions
Name calling
Using a harsh and degrading tone of voice

Psychological and Emotional Abuse

Humiliates you in front of others
Prevents or discourages you from seeing family or friends
Threatens to hurt you or people you care about
Threatens to harm herself when upset with you
Controls how you spend your money
Unfairly accuses you of being unfaithful
Put-downs
Blaming you
Dismissing your feelings

Are any of the above behaviors a problem in your household?

Develop a Safety Plan

It is important to make a plan to keep yourself and your children safe, even if your LO has never been violent. You may never need to use it, but like an insurance policy, it's important to have it if you do need it. Here are some things to consider:

- Pack a bag and keep it in a safe location (not in your home). Examples of things to include: clothing, money, personal documents, legal documents, extra keys, medications. See "Other Potential Sources of Support" (p.90) for a more extensive list.

- Tell neighbors about the abuse and have them call the police if they hear noise coming from your house.

- Talk to your children about how they can keep themselves safe as well.

- Nominate a safe house – preferably not a close friend's or relative's as this is the first place your LO may come to find you. If you do not have a suitable location then find out where the nearest shelter or police station is. See "Other Potential Sources of Support" (p.90) for additional resources.

- Psychological and verbal abuse, such as put-downs, intimidation, bullying and threats, can also be harmful. Protect yourself by setting boundaries, removing yourself from the situation, talking about it to others, and nurturing yourself.

- Learn to recognize "red flags": "Red flags" are warning signs that indicate that violent behavior may be escalating. Work through the exercises in Chapter 3 of *Get Your Loved One Sober* to identify common "red flags" specific to your relationship with your LO. E.g., your LO starts talking to you with an irritable tone of voice, starts becoming agitated, slams doors, etc.

- Diffuse the situation if possible. When you observe a "red flag", this should be your cue to protect yourself by managing your own responses . Although it may be difficult to change how you respond to your LO it is not impossible. Work through the exercises in Chapter 3 of *Get Your Loved One Sober* to script your responses to "red flags" when you see them. E.g., keeping your voice calm, walking away, going into another room. Using Positive or Understanding statements. (see Section 6: Positive Communication)

- Decide in advance at what point you need to call the police. What is the red flag that indicates you need to call for help? E.g., you may decide that you will call the police if you are threatened with violence or abuse.

© 2012 SMART Recovery® - All Rights Reserved

Developing a Support Network

It is common for families of someone with a drug or alcohol problem to become isolated. Often, out of shame or a sense of social stigma, families try to hide the reality of their situation from their friends and family.

They may stop inviting people over because of the unpredictable and sometimes volatile behavior of their Loved One.

The result of isolation can be increased stress, reduced ability to cope, loss of perspective on what is "normal" or acceptable. This may also include mental health problems, such as depression and anxiety. Having a support network is another important way of looking after yourself.

The following exercise will guide you through a systematic way of identifying and connecting with supportive people in your life.

"The greatest healing therapy is friendship and love." ~Hubert H. Humphrey, Jr.

Developing a Support Network

- Think about *all the people you know*, including family, friends and acquaintances.

- Among those are likely to be some that you feel close to, some who you enjoy socializing with and some with whom you wouldn't choose to spend any more time with than you have to.

- If you cross the last group off the list, you are left with people who you might like to spend time with on a casual basis and (hopefully) at least one with whom you could talk about your situation.

1. List people that you could contact for a social occasion, such as coffee, lunch or a movie.

2. Choose at least one person and identify how, when and what you could invite them to do with you. Be specific. E.g., *call/text/email Sharon and ask if she would like to meet for coffee next Tuesday.*

3. Are there any unhelpful thoughts that might get in the way of you being able to do this? E.g., *"I might be rejected"* or *"I might look desperate, as if I have no friends"*

   © 2012 SMART Recovery® - All Rights Reserved

4. Can you challenge these unhelpful thoughts, using REBT? E.g., replacing the above unhelpful belief ("I might be rejected") with a more helpful one, such as: *"If someone asks me out for a coffee, I usually feel flattered. If she doesn't want to come she can say no and I will cope."*

5. List anyone who might be a potential source of emotional support –
i.e., someone who will listen to you without judging or telling you what to do.

6. If you have been able to identify someone, think about how you might reach out to them. E.g., *"I will call my sister and ask if we can find a time to meet and talk about something that is bothering me."*

7. What unhelpful thoughts might get in the way of you being able to do this? E.g., *"I don't want to burden her with my problems."*

8. How can you challenge these unhelpful thoughts, using REBT? E.g., replacing the above unhelpful belief ("I don't want to burden her with my problems") with a more helpful one, such as:*"She is my sister and she cares about me, just as I care about her."*

Other Potential Sources of Support

- **NNEDV: National Network to End Domestic Violence** – website provides many resources including information on the many forms of domestic violence and an extensive list of things to have readily available to you if you need to depart quickly. *http://nnedv.org/resources/stats/gethelp.html*

- **Women's Law**: provides legal information and support for victims of domestic violence *http://www.womenslaw.org*

- **Dial 211** – for information on resources available in your community *http://211us.org*

- **Dial 911** – for emergency help

- **Individual Counseling**

- **SMART Recovery Family & Friends** - Science-based, self-help, peer-support incorporating SMART Recovery tools and concepts *http://www.smartrecovery.org/family*

- **Al-Anon and Nar-Anon** - Self-help support groups (12-step) for families and friends of people with addiction

© 2012 SMART Recovery® - All Rights Reserved

Coping with Lapses

Implementing lifestyle changes is hard work and few people do it perfectly.

As discussed in a previous section, change is a *process*, not an event. Lapses and relapses are a natural part of the change process. They can occur when someone is trying to change any behavior. Lapses and relapses often occur in the change process of someone giving up addiction...and lapses and relapses often occur when someone is making other behavioral changes (e.g., changing habitual responses to a Loved One's addiction, such as "nagging, pleading and threatening").

Learning how to effectively respond to your own setbacks in making changes to your habitual responses to your LO, is a key to successful change.

The difference between someone who gets "stuck" and finds their lapse turning into a full-blown relapse, and someone who gets back on track quickly, lies in how they *interpret* the lapse. Lapses can be interpreted as failures or they can be viewed as *opportunities* to learn what didn't work, and to plan more effective strategies for dealing with similar circumstances in the future.

Maintaining motivation in the face of lapses and relapses is also an important component in any effective change process.

Lapse vs. Relapse

What is a lapse?

A lapse is a temporary set-back in the process of changing your behavior. It is an occasion, or number of occasions, when you have been unable to stick to your goals for change and have gone back to your habitual way(s) of responding to your Loved One's (LO's) addictive behaviors.

Examples:

Self-Care: If you have committed to adding a 30 minute walk to your day as a part of your self-care plan and find yourself distracted by other things and "forgetting" about the walk, that would be considered a lapse.

Communication: If you have committed to using a positive (PIUS) communication style when talking to your LO about a problem and then find yourself getting into a heated argument about the problem, that would be considered a lapse.

Boundaries: As a part of developing healthy boundaries for yourself, you may have committed to removing yourself when your LO comes home intoxicated. If your LO comes home intoxicated and instead of following your boundary plan and removing yourself, you instead get angry and yell at your LO, that would be considered a lapse.

What is a relapse?

Unlike a lapse, which is temporary, a relapse is when we lose sight of our goals for change and return to our old habits. Relapse involves a change in our state of mind. Sometimes we give up on the changes we were trying to make because it seems too hard to keep going. We may eventually give up completely on the new behavior, especially if we aren't seeing any significant positive results of our efforts. Consequently, a relapse lasts much longer than a lapse.

If we have an occasion or occasions of resorting to reacting/behaving in old unhelpful ways, *but we are still committed* to trying to develop new, more helpful behaviors, this would be considered a lapse, rather than a relapse.

However, repeated or prolonged lapses tend to lead to relapses, so it is important to take steps early to get back on track following a lapse.

What does it mean if I have a lapse? Am I doomed to a relapse?

Often lapses occur when we encounter a situation that we cannot manage using our new strategies. This may happen because:

- We planned for a situation, but the situation didn't end up being as we expected it, or we were unable to put our plan into action.

- We couldn't plan for a situation, because the situation was unexpected.

- We didn't plan for a situation, because we had been doing well for a while and thought we'd be okay.

Having a lapse doesn't mean we have failed. It's simply a signal that we need to be prepared to handle the situation better the next time it occurs.

Managing lapses

If you should have a lapse, remember to watch your self-talk (see Section 3: Inner Dialogue). Beating yourself up over the incident tends to be counter-productive and may lead to further lapses. If you feel so angry or disappointed in yourself that you start saying things like *"I'm hopeless, I might as well give up"* this will probably make it more difficult to move forward and get back on track. Remember, you are human and therefore not 100% perfect, so why would your behavior be?!

Lapses are learning opportunities

Instead of beating yourself up, you might choose to view a lapse as a learning experience. First, accept what happened, and then work out why it happened and what you could do differently next time. Some of the skills and strategies you've been working on with SMART Family & Friends may be of assistance with this.

It is not possible to guarantee that you will never experience a lapse. Lapses are a natural part of the process of changing. One of the best things you can do is to make a plan for what to do if you *do* have a lapse. People who have a plan for dealing with a lapse are much less likely to relapse.

"If you don't make mistakes, you aren't really trying." ~- Coleman Hawkins

© 2012 SMART Recovery® - All Rights Reserved

Coping with Lapses

It can be helpful to have a plan for how to deal with a lapse, even if you never need to use it. The following steps can help you get back on track and avoid a relapse.

1. Challenge any self-defeating thoughts

Examine your thoughts about the lapse using REBT strategies for challenging unhelpful beliefs. Below is an example, using the scenario of getting angry and yelling at your Loved One when she came home intoxicated, rather than sticking to your boundary plan of removing yourself:

Unhelpful Thought	Evidence For	Evidence Against	More Helpful Thought
I'm so hopeless. I'll never be able to figure out how to deal with this situation. I might as well give up!	I wasn't able to control my anger.	I've been successful in lots of other situations. This was just one slip-up.	*I've been doing well controlling my anger and looking after myself in lots of situations up until now. This was just a slip-up.*

2. Identify why the lapse happened

There is usually a trigger for a lapse. Think about:

- What was going on before the lapse occurred? It may be something that happened (e.g., I had an argument with my partner earlier in the day). It may be a feeling you had (e.g., being tired or stressed over work events).

    Were you unprepared for the situation that happened?

    Did your plan not work for some reason?

3. Think about what you could have done differently

It may help to use problem-solving skills (see GYLOS ch 8) to develop a plan for dealing with similar situations differently next time.

4. Get extra support if you need to

Sometimes lapses can be a sign that you need extra support. It is better to seek extra help after a lapse than to keep struggling by yourself and risk having your lapse develop into a relapse. Use some of the contacts in your support network. (See Section 8: Safety and Support)

Maintaining Motivation

Behavior change is almost never easy. It can be difficult to maintain your motivation for change, especially in the aftermath of a lapse or when you see no visible results of your efforts.

> *"People often say that motivation doesn't last. Well, neither does bathing —*
> *that's why we recommend it daily."* ~Zig Ziglar

To help maintain your motivation it can be helpful to revisit your original reasons for wanting to change, review your progress so far, and your goals for the future.

Answer the following questions:

What were your original reasons for making a change?

What results have you noticed so far?

How have these results affected your life?

What might the future look like if you continue to work towards change?

Why is this important to you?

What might the future look like if you stop working toward change?

How do you feel about this?

What will help to keep you motivated?

Remember: Change requires Practice, Patience, Persistence

 © 2012 SMART Recovery® - All Rights Reserved

Additional Resources

"Get Your Loved One Sober" — Chapter 12: Relapse Prevention

"We are not suggesting you permanently take on all the work of the relationship. Indeed, the long-term goals here are that you have less work to do in keeping the family running and that your Loved One becomes an involved, responsible family member. Between now and then, however, you will need to put out extra effort. Besides, our guess is that you are already doing most of the work anyhow. This is a continuation of that state of affairs but with a better long-term outcome." ~ GYLOS

NOTES

Disable the Enabling

Resign Your Job as Manager of Your Loved One's Addiction

As you have tried to help your Loved One (LO) toward recovery, you may have found yourself taking on the role of "Manager", attempting to manage the addiction in various ways.

This section explores how to identify any of your coping and helping behaviors that may fall under the umbrella of "enabling". These are often behaviors that were well-intentioned when they began, but which may not be working well now.

It can be helpful to gain awareness and insight about how certain strategies which you intended as helpful, are actually counter-productive. From there you can better explore the choices available to you for changing any unhelpful strategies to more helpful ones.

If what you are doing is not working, you may want to consider your options for "resigning your job as manager of your LO's addiction".

Enabling Behaviors

No one wants to think that they are acting in ways that enable or make it easier for their Loved One (LO) to continue their addiction. But as the addiction progresses, our well-intentioned "helping actions" often evolve into "enabling behaviors":

Enabling: To prevent a person from experiencing NATURAL consequences of their behavior by *changing* the consequences — or by *accepting responsibility* for them.

Enabling: Doing anything for the other person that they CAN AND SHOULD be doing for themselves.

We can't change our LO's behaviors, we can only change our own. But because our lives intersect with our LO's lives, we do have some ability, through our interactions with our LO, to influence his/her choices — positively or negatively.   There is no guarantee our LO will choose recovery, but we can do our best to increase the likelihood of our LO making some better choices by making recovery more appealing than addiction (see GYLOS Ch 2 & 8) and **by making addiction as unappealing as possible (see GYLOS Ch 7)**

We can make addiction as unappealing as possible by examining **our** behaviors and changing them so that we are not reinforcing the addiction in any way. In other words, we want to "disable the enabling".

If nothing changes, nothing changes.

We have the *"POWER OF CHOICE"*. We can look at how we interact with our LO to see if we may be doing things that are keeping him/her from facing the real consequences of his addiction. And then it is up to us to CHOOSE: to make changes in our behavior — or to stay the course.

"What starts out as helping, turns into relationship poison." ~GYLOS

It can be disconcerting to think that our behaviors have contributed to the problem, but remember that most of us have not had any training in this sort of thing. Many "enabling behaviors" are often "normal behaviors" that, for the most part, work just fine in healthy relationships; they just backfire in a relationship that involves someone with a chemical dependency. Your original efforts to help were well-intentioned. You were doing the best you could with the information and life experience you had at the time you became aware of the addiction.   Once you have new information about addiction and enabling you may wish to make different choices.

"If you want them to improve, if you really want to help your drinker,
you must stop protecting them." ~GYLOS

© 2012 SMART Recovery® - All Rights Reserved

Enabling Questionnaire

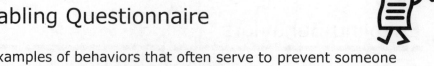

The questions below are examples of behaviors that often serve to prevent someone from experiencing the natural consequences and repercussions of their choices to continue with the addiction rather than to choose recovery.

True or False:

_____Have you paid bills that your Loved One (LO) was supposed to have paid?

_____Do you avoid talking about your LO's drinking or drugging out of fear of the response?

_____Have you threatened to leave if your LO didn't stop drinking — and then _did not_ leave?

_____Have you woken your LO so that she would not be late for work or school?

_____Have you explained (multiple times) to your LO that he MUST stop drinking/using?

_____Have you bailed your LO out of jail or paid her legal fees?

_____Have you ever helped your LO look for items he lost while drinking or using?

_____Have you ever avoided making plans to spend time with family or friends because you were concerned your LO's behavior would be unpleasant due to drugs or drinking?

_____Have you ever cut back on your own expenses due to your LO's substance use?

_____Do you believe your LO's lies — over and over?

_____Do you accept your LO's excuses?

_____Do you allow yourself to be physically or emotionally abused by your LO?

_____Do you make addictive behavior seem "normal" to your children?

_____Do you let your LO change the subject when you bring up their substance abuse problem?

_____Do you nag/plead/threaten your LO in an effort to inspire change?

_____Do you keep your LO's addiction a secret from others? To protect your LO? To protect other family members from the uncomfortable truth? To avoid feeling embarrassed for yourself?

> _Your words may be to the contrary, as you scold, nag, beg, plead,_
> _but your behavior shouts: "I'm here to make it easier for you ." ~GYLOS_

  © 2012 SMART Recovery® - All Rights Reserved

Disabling the Enabling

"Enabling behaviors" generally fall into one of three categories:

Fixing problems: e.g., calling in sick for a LO who can't work due to "using"

Protecting your LO: e.g., covering up for her with family, making excuses, keeping the real problem a secret

Nagging: e.g., frequently reminding your LO of "the problem" and urging him to do something about it

The problem with these behaviors and strategies is that they either prevent your Loved One from having to deal with the consequences of their addiction, OR ....

Your LO uses all his/her energy to respond to you and your reactions *and not the addiction*. If we look at things from the LO's point of view, he doesn't have a problem with *drinking or using*, he has a problem with *YOU*!!

Enabling behaviors are unhelpful for everyone involved — they have long-term consequences that are the *opposite of what you are intending*. They allow the addiction to continue at the expense of your emotional, physical and financial resources. When that happens, it can often lead to negative emotions. If you find yourself feeling frustrated, angry, resentful, sad, hopeless or depressed, it may well be that changing your interaction with your Loved One is a good idea, for you and for her.

If you think that you *might* be enabling your LO in some way, review your typical interactions with your LO. Look for ways in which you may be Fixing, Nagging or Protecting.

If you've been fixing, protecting or nagging for some time, chances are you now have a *habit* of doing so that you may want to break. He drinks/uses and you feel compelled to nag. She creates a problem and you feel compelled to fix it. He hides his addiction from the world and you protect him and hide the addiction, too.

Consider a lighthouse. It stands on the shore with its beckoning light, guiding ships safely into the harbor. The lighthouse can't uproot itself, wade out into the water, grab the ship by the stern and say, "listen you fool — if you stay on this path you will break up on the rocks".

No. The ship has some responsibility for its own destiny. It can choose to be guided by the light in the lighthouse. Or, it can go its own way. The lighthouse is not responsible for the ship's decisions. All it can do is be the best lighthouse it knows how to be.

Use the following worksheets to identify any Nagging, Fixing or Protecting behaviors you wish to change.

Disabling the Enabling

How can you overcome your impulses to fix, nag, and protect?

Start by making a list of specific things that you do that you suspect may be enabling. Now that you are aware of some behaviors that you might want to change,

Ask Yourself:

1. Why am I doing these things? What am I telling myself about this situation that has been making it ok for me to do these things? Some things that you may be telling yourself:

> My Loved One (LO) *needs* my help (and I MUST help her)
> I can't be happy until my LO changes
> It hurts me to see this
> I'm the only one my LO trusts to help him fight this addiction

2. Has my behavior been effective in solving the problem?

3. What's stopping me from changing my enabling behaviors? For example:

> I don't want to hurt my LO
> He/she will be angry with me
> It's going to hurt ME to no longer protect my child
> I just don't see how it will make any difference

4. Challenge your reasons for continuing your enabling behaviors:

> Will disabling the enabling truly hurt my LO? Yes, she may get angry, but what is that in comparison to the long-term HARM of addiction that I am working to avoid?
> What will hurt ME more: disabling the enabling, or knowing that I didn't do everything I could?
> What can I expect to happen if I *don't change*? Will things get better?

5. Choose an enabling behavior that you'd like to change. Use the *Change Plan Worksheet* to plan how you will implement your change. Consider which SMART tools might be helpful to you in planning your new behavior (e.g., positive communication, assertive communication, healthy boundaries).

Expected Outcome of Allowing Natural Consequences

Can you expect your LO to pursue recovery as soon as you discontinue any enabling behaviors? Unfortunately, there are no guarantees that your LO will seek recovery, no matter what course of action you choose to take. If you do change your behaviors to eliminate any and all enabling, it is even possible that the situation may appear to get worse before it gets better.

Changing how you interact with your LO will feel uncomfortable at first. This is normal. Remember just because your new behavior may FEEL wrong, that doesn't mean it IS wrong. Congratulate yourself for the really hard working you're doing, keep your eye on your goals and remember the Three P's: Be PATIENT with yourself, PRACTICE what you are learning here and be PERSISTANT.

    © 2012 SMART Recovery® - All Rights Reserved

Change Plan Worksheet

Planning is a key to making successful changes. Use this worksheet to develop your own plan for making a change in your behavior.

1. The change I want to make is:

2. The most important reasons why I want to make this change are:

3. The steps I plan to take in making this change are:

4. The ways other people can help me are:

   Person: Possible ways to help me:

5. I will know that my plan is working if:

6. Some things that could interfere with my plans are:

7. How important is it that I make this change:

Not important										*Very important*
0	1	2	3	4	5	6	7	8	9	10

8. How confident am I that I can make this change?

Not confident										*Very confident*
0	1	2	3	4	5	6	7	8	9	10

Additional Resources

"Get Your Loved One Sober" — Chapter 7: Disable the Enabling

Supporting Recovery Without Enabling
by Tom Horvath, Ph.D. *https://goo.gl/8XNfyE*

Thoughts on Compassion and Enabling:

One problem that many Family & Friends have in finding the motivation to stop their enabling behaviors, is that they perceive their enabling behaviors as acts of compassion, intended to alleviate discomfort and suffering of their Loved One. And the enabling behaviors (nagging, pleading and threatening) often *do appear* to work — at least *in the short-term*. Unfortunately, they also allow the problem to continue and to get worse *in the long-term*.

If we assume that true compassion includes the desire to alleviate the LO's discomfort and suffering *in the long-term*, then we can conclude that, in fact, *enabling is the <u>opposite</u> of true compassion*.

Thoughts on Enabling Behaviors and Addictive Behaviors:

Enabling and addiction have something in common. Both are *non-helpful coping strategies*. They both provide a "quick-fix, short-term, feel-good solution" that creates long-term problems. Family & Friends would do well to consider healthier coping strategies to replace the enabling, just as their LO would do well to consider healthier coping strategies to replace the addiction.

© 2012 SMART Recovery® - All Rights Reserved

Healthy Boundaries Part II

Protecting Your Boundaries

What are your choices if you have identified and communicated a boundary with your Loved One (LO) — and you are ignored?

We are each responsible for "protecting" our own boundaries. In other words, if asking nicely isn't getting the result you wanted, you have a choice to make: back off and choose to live with the behavior, or move on to the next phase of boundary work: boundary protection. Your choice, no matter what it is, influences the likelihood of your LO choosing to respect your boundaries — or not.

What message do you send to your LO when you communicate a boundary and then *protect it* when it crossed?

What message do you send to your LO when you communicate a boundary and then *fail to protect it* when it is crossed?

If you do choose to protect your boundaries, how can you do this in an effective and respectful way?

This section on Healthy Boundaries (Part II) is a guide to finding your own answers to these questions.

Boundaries Require Protection to Be Effective

In a perfect world, everyone communicates their boundaries calmly and clearly, and those around them respect their requests for "appropriate behavior" (and they all live happily ever after).

Formula for communicating a boundary request

> **Inform:** When you do: (*YOUR BEHAVIOR*), I feel: (*MY REACTION*)
> **Request:** Can I ask you to (*STOP or CHANGE this BEHAVIOR*)?

Since we don't live in a perfect world, others sometimes do choose to disregard our boundary requests and the "inappropriate behavior" continues. If this happens, it may be beneficial to clearly and calmly restate a boundary request several times over a period of days or weeks. *Reminder:* Boundaries communicated to a Loved One who is intoxicated may not be "heard" or remembered.

If a boundary is continually ignored, even after repeated requests, then we have a responsibility *to ourselves* to *protect* the boundary, not just one time, but *every* time , *from now on*. Remember: Actions speak louder than words. *Consistency of our actions is the best way to protect a boundary.*

Formula for communicating a planned protective action, if a boundary request continues to be ignored:

> **Inform:** When you do: (*YOUR BEHAVIOR*), I feel: (*MY REACTION*)
> **Request:** Can I ask you to (*STOP or CHANGE this BEHAVIOR*)?
>
> **Inform:** If you are not willing to(*STOP or CHANGE this BEHAVIOR*)?, I will need to (*TAKE PROTECTIVE ACTION*).

Example:

> **Inform:** When you raise your voice, it hurts me — and it scares the children.

> **Request:** I've asked you several times over the last few weeks to speak in a normal volume when you talk to me or the kids, but nothing has changed.

> **Inform:** From now on, when you raise your voice, the kids and I will go to grandma's for the evening.

Keeping it Positive:

In really significant boundary conversations when you are confronting someone about a serious problem (e.g., "I'm concerned that your drinking is out of control") it can be helpful to set the tone for the conversation by starting off with positive statements that affirm and validate how important your relationship with the other person is:

> Example: *John, I want you to know that the reason I'm bringing this up is because I love you and I am committed to our relationship. I love and value so many things about you. In fact, that is why I have to talk to you about this.*

Protective Action

When first learning about boundaries, Family & Friends sometimes confuse the actions needed to protect a boundary with making a choice to punish the LO for their actions. It may be helpful to recall that GYLOS does not recommend "punishment" and points out that punishments often backfire. Instead, they suggest a simple and powerful action for protecting your boundary: disengage, remove yourself from the situation. In many cases, some variation of "disengage" is sufficient to communicate the seriousness of your boundary request.

The first time you find yourself communicating your plan to take protective action you may not have had time to decide what you're going to do — In that case, you may just state, calmly, matter-of-factly, "if you're not willing to do this, I'll need to make some decisions about what I'm going to do."

 © 2012 SMART Recovery® - All Rights Reserved

Planning a Boundary Request

Using the Boundary Request Formula (Inform, Request, Inform) plan a boundary request for each of the following scenarios:

1. When my Loved One (LO) is actively engaged with her addiction, she is disagreeable and unpleasant to be around — or she's passed out. In response, I waver between anger, despair and sadness.

2. When my LO is actively engaged with his addiction, he often fails to show up for things we have planned and sometimes disappears for hours (or days) at a time. In response, I feel frustrated and hurt at his disrespectful behaviors.

3. When my LO is actively using, he sometimes steals from me. In response I feel angry and also sad, knowing that he cannot be trusted.

4. I wish my wife did not drink so much when I am at work. I know she sometimes drinks until she's passed out. I am scared that she cannot wake up when the baby is crying or that my older child will not be able to wake her and will think that she is dead. I wish she would not drink with the kids around.

© 2012 SMART Recovery® - All Rights Reserved

Role of Boundaries in Healthy Relationships

Healthy relationships happen when we actively **and consistently respect** each other's rights and preferences. They are based on equality and mutual respect. They are based on healthy boundaries.

All relationships have boundaries and when they are respected, the need for continual reminders about those boundaries is rarely necessary. But when problems arise (such as addiction and the behaviors that come with it), it becomes necessary to make the boundaries clear. It becomes necessary to let the other person know that their behavior is disrespectful, or harmful, and that you don't want it to continue.

Some examples of behavior that you may find unacceptable:

LO borrowing money he cannot or do not pay back

LO expecting financial support from you while she spends her money on the addiction

LO lying in any way to cover up the truth of his activities

LO taking long absences or putting lives at risk by drinking and driving

My Boundaries Cannot *Make You* Do Anything

As much as we *want* our LO to stop the behaviors related to the addiction, it's important to understand that the purpose of boundaries is *not* to punish the other person or manipulate them into changing.

The truth is that one person's boundary *cannot make* another person change. It may give them *good reason to choose* to change, but they retain their own "power of choice". We may not like it if they choose not to change, but we would do well to accept that they have a right to choose for themselves.

Our power of choice includes our ability to let others know how their behaviors are impacting us and to offer them a chance to stop the damage to our relationship before it is too late — before things get to a point where we have to build a WALL instead of a boundary. We do this by taking responsibility for **calmly, clearly and consistently communicating** our boundaries.

WALLS are for keeping people out. Hopefully with **effective, healthy** boundaries you won't find yourself needing walls to keep your Loved One out of your life.

Reminder: Protecting your boundaries is not a way to punish others or manipulate them into complying with your wishes. It is not a sign of disrespect for others' needs. It is a sign of respect for yourself and for the relationship.

     © 2012 SMART Recovery® - All Rights Reserved

Boundaries: An Antidote for Enabling

Disable the Enabling

As discussed in Section 10 fixing, protecting and nagging, are not helpful, and often have the effect of enabling, or allowing, the addiction to continue.

If the communication in our relationship with our LO has deteriorated to the point where we are frequently nagging, pleading, and arguing, we may want to choose a different method of communicating, especially since these methods have been shown to contribute to an environment that enables the addiction. It is not easy to change communication styles, but it can be done. We *can* learn to communicate in a different way.

Positive communication, assertive communication and boundaries are effective tools we can use to communicate honestly and clearly. They are tools we can use (instead of nagging, pleading and arguing) to let others in our lives know what behaviors are acceptable and which are not acceptable — *to us*.

Rather than the drama of nagging, pleading and threatening, we can use these tools to *show* our LO **clearly, calmly, and consistently** that his behavior is not acceptable and THEN WE LEAVE IT UP TO HIM to decide what, if anything, he wants to do about it. In other words, by communicating our boundaries, we meet *our responsibility* for "disabling the enabling" and allow *our LO to become fully responsible* for the problem.

Hurt vs. Harm

Enabling behaviors and addiction have something in common. Both are "quick-fix, short-term solutions". They have the desired effect (minimizing pain or discomfort) but only in the short-term and they have negative long-term consequences. Yes, there is often some discomfort (hurt) involved in protecting boundaries that your LO is ignoring. Whatever action you have chosen to take in order to protect your boundary (usually disengaging in some way) can be painful for your LO. It may also be painful for you. However, the action you take to protect your boundaries, as uncomfortable as it feels in the moment, is minor compared to the *lasting harm that is caused by addiction*. Like someone with addiction, *you have a choice:* continue on the path of short-term gratification or take the more difficult, but more rewarding, path to long-term recovery.

"The chief cause of failure and unhappiness is trading what you want most for what you want right now."~Zig Ziglar

5 Steps to Establish *Healthy* Boundaries

In order to establish healthy boundaries between yourself and others:

1. Identify the symptoms of your boundaries currently being, or having been, violated or ignored. Some symptoms to look for: anger, frustration, feeling powerless or hopeless

> Example: "My partner is often late for dinner and I'm *sick and tired* of eating alone."

2. Take responsibility for your own upsets. Identify the irrational or unhealthy thinking and beliefs which are fueling any high drama (anger, frustration, anxiety, sadness) you are experiencing over the behaviors. The ABC tool (Section 4) and Exchange Vocabulary (Section 3) can be very helpful for this.

3. Identify new, more rational, healthy thinking and beliefs. Rational, healthy thinking will lead to less anger and frustration in your life and put you in a better position to communicate your boundaries — calmly, clearly and consistently.

> Example: "Rather than staying quiet in order to avoid conflict, I will stand up for myself so that my Loved One can learn to respect my rights and my needs in the relationship."

4. Identify any new skills (e.g., assertive communication) you want to work on in order to sustain healthy boundaries between you and your Loved One. The key word there is "sustain". Like fences, personal boundaries require maintenance.

5. Implement healthy boundary-building beliefs and behaviors in your life.

<u>Healthy Boundary Building Behaviors:</u> Managing the need for approval, managing fear of rejection, improving assertive communication skills, developing self-control, setting goals

<u>Healthy boundary building beliefs:</u>

I have the right to ask for what I want.
I have the right to have my needs and wants respected by others.
I have the right to be treated with dignity and respect.
I have the right to be happy.
I have the right to express all of my feelings, positive or negative.
I have the right to follow my own values and standards.
I have the right not to be responsible for my LO's behavior, actions, feelings or problems.
I have the right to expect honesty from others.
I have the right not to give excuses or reasons for my behavior.
I have the right to make decisions based on my feelings.
I have the right to be in a non-abusive environment.
I have the right to feel safe in my own home.

Adapted from Dr. James J. Messina's "Healthy Boundaries" at www.coping.us

© 2012 SMART Recovery® - All Rights Reserved

Tips for Setting Boundaries

- **Remember WHY we make boundary requests:** Boundary requests _are_ an effective way to say "this is important to me — please pay attention." Boundary requests _are not_ a way to punish your LO for unwanted behavior.

- **Start small:** Build up your boundary skills by starting with small requests, delivered to others (not your LO) to gain experience and confidence.

- **Delivery:** Boundaries are best delivered using positive and assertive (not aggressive) communication. Consider using the PIUS communication model described in Chapter 9 of GYLOS.

- **Timing:** Boundary requests benefit from being planned ahead of time. They are best shared with your LO when _you_ are feeling calm and clear and when your LO is sober.

- **3C's of Boundary Communication:** Be CALM, Be CLEAR, Be CONSISTENT.

    CALM: Boundaries are best delivered respectfully and matter-of-factly.

    CLEAR: Straightforward communication without extraneous explaining.

    CONSISTENT: Stay on message and follow through with your plan to protect your boundaries as needed. Every. Single. Time.

- **Prepare to be challenged:** Your LO may verbally challenge your boundary, claiming it is unfair or harsh. Your boundaries represent _your personal preferences_. You have a right to hold and express personal preferences and _you are not obligated to defend their merits_. Remember that boundaries are CLEAR communication about _what you want_ and _what you intend to do_ to protect the boundary if it is not honored. Your LO has a choice to honor your request — or not. Attempts to argue with you about the merits of your boundary may best be deferred by simply repeating the boundary, _calmly, clearly and consistently_.

- **Plan to protect the boundary:** Your LO may forget your boundary request or may not take it seriously. Know that this is relatively common and be prepared to follow through on your plan to protect your boundary, as needed. Every. Single. Time.

- **Lead by example:** Model the kind of behavior you expect. For example, if you don't want your son or daughter to take drugs at home, don't use drugs or alcohol yourself. If you don't want your spouse to drink, don't drink yourself.

- **Respect is a two-way street:** Your LO has boundaries, too. Honoring your LO's boundaries sets the tone in the relationship and increases the likelihood that your LO will respect your boundary requests.

NOTES

Trust and Forgiveness

Addictive behaviors typically include deception, false promises, broken promises and dishonest behaviors. You may want to believe what your Loved One (LO) wants you to believe: that he is all right, that the addiction is not a problem, that she didn't take money from your purse, that this time, he really is quitting. But over time, as you uncover deceptions and experience broken promises again and again, the evidence that your LO is not entirely trustworthy may become overwhelming. You may quite possibly find that the untrustworthy behaviors extend beyond the addiction and affect other areas of your life with your LO.

This section explores ways that Family & Friends can deal with broken trust, rebuilding trust, and letting go of past hurts.

Trust

Lost trust is a common issue for Family & Friends (F&F) of a Loved One (LO) with an addiction. They experience feelings of disappointment, frustration, hurt and anger over the LO's behaviors. They may find themselves walking on eggshells, unable to trust their ability to predict their LO's emotional responses. They may be concerned for their financial security or their physical safety as they are unable to trust their LO to be respectful of their needs in these areas. The consistently unreliable and untruthful communication that often accompanies addiction has an enormous emotional impact on F&F, one that takes a long time to heal.

Expectations and Acceptance

For F&F to hold on to an expectation that they *should be able to trust* their LO who has an addiction or is in early recovery, is unrealistic and a recipe for disappointment. A more realistic view is to accept that once broken, trust takes a long time to rebuild and that rebuilding is the responsibility of the LO, not the F&F.

Recovery, Hope and Trust

Early recovery does restore hope, but hope and trust are not the same thing.

It can be very challenging for F&F, and for the LO in recovery, to balance the LO's desire to be trusted in their recovery efforts, with the very real need for F&F to *fully accept the reality* that not every recovery attempt will be 100% successful or 100% immediate. F&F would also do well to *fully accept* that even though "using" has stopped, some old behaviors may linger. It may be some time before the LO is willing, or able, to address the changes needed to rebuild trust in the relationship.

Rebuilding trust is not an easy task. After engaging in sometimes years of addiction-related activities and behaviors that have taught their F&F that they cannot be trusted, it is not realistic for a LO to expect to rebuild trust quickly.

"The Trust Bank "

It may help to think of trust in the relationship the way you would think of a bank account. We are each responsible for our own account.

Each thoughtful act, each personal communication, each time we keep our word and follow through on our commitments is a deposit into the account. Likewise each broken promise, hurtful comment, lie or misrepresentation is a withdrawal.

Your LO may have been making small deposits over the years, but with addiction the withdrawals become larger and larger and your LO's account may now be overdrawn. At this point, the trust is lost completely — but not necessarily forever. Over time, with many deposits and few, or no, withdrawals a positive balance can be restored.

Since we are each responsible for our own account, it is not possible for a F&F to make deposits into the LO's account. That is the LO's job. Only your LO can add to the account or subtract from it. If your LO chooses to work on rebuilding his trust account, it will take a long time (often years) to restore a healthy balance, just as it would to recover from any bankruptcy.

Trust Building

Rebuilding trust is an area where good, positive communication *on an ongoing basis* is required. Your Loved One (LO) cannot read your mind and will not know what you need to feel confident in trusting again, unless you communicate that. The more specific you can be the better.

Remember to acknowledge your LO's deposits into the trust account — reinforce the behaviors (truthfulness, integrity, reliability) that you want to see more of in your relationship.

Use the space below to list some ways that your LO can make deposits into the Trust Bank.

Think about what *you* need from your LO in order for you to be able to begin trusting again. Use the space below to record your thoughts.

© 2012 SMART Recovery® - All Rights Reserved

Acceptance & Forgiveness

Throughout this Handbook, we have presented tools for managing extreme emotions that may interfere with our ability to function well in our lives.

Acceptance

Another powerful tool for improving our ability to function and be happy is the one of Acceptance. Often we stay stuck in our emotional upsets because we do not know how to resolve the gap between our expectations and what is actually happening. We may have an expectation that our child will grow up to lead a happy and productive life and when that doesn't happen, the gap between our expectations and the reality of our child's choices is difficult for us to resolve. We may have an expectation that our spouse will be a loving and supportive partner, only to be dismayed by the reality that addiction makes that difficult or impossible. We stay stuck, waiting for something to change to resolve the situation.

It seems paradoxical, but "acceptance of what is" is a prerequisite for change. Acceptance should not be confused with approval. It *does not* imply liking the situation, or being willing to continue allowing it to be a part of your life. It *does* mean accepting the reality of the situation or the other person's behavior, no matter how objectionable. Once you have accepted the reality of the situation, you are in a much better position to deal with it effectively, creatively, positively and in a way that best benefits you.

Forgiveness

The Importance of Forgiveness: What happens when we cannot let go of anger and resentment? We may spend countless hours reliving past events and harboring grudges. We may hold on to feelings of blame, where we blame our Loved One (LO) for our upset feelings. These thoughts keep us trapped in the role of the victim as we continue to focus on how our LO has hurt us. Since our emotional energy is focused on the past, we remain powerless to move forward. Over time, the failure to achieve resolution of our anger and resentment takes a physical and emotional toll. Continually thinking about past events can lead to self-defeating behaviors (angry outbursts, retaliation, addiction, avoidance) and high levels of emotional arousal that can ultimately contribute to serious medical problems (e.g., heart disease).

Learning to accept, to forgive, and to let go of past hurts is not easy, but neither is living your life stuck in anger and resentment.

Exploring the Option of Forgiveness

If you are holding on to past hurts or anger, consider forgiveness as a way to move forward. Forgiveness is not a quick fix. It's a matter of a willed change in our thinking about our own demands that others treat us in a certain way — or else!

Think about an incident that has left you feeling angry or hurt and that you have had trouble "letting go".

1. How does my anger benefit me?

2. What are some reasons to keep being angry?

3. How much time and effort does it take to keep the anger going? And does it help me?

4. How does my anger hurt me?

5. What might happen to my anger if I could stop having thoughts of how to correct the unfairness, or even of how to just get my Loved One to apologize?

6. If I decide to make a direct and conscious decision to forgive, what benefits might I gain?

7. Is it possible that with less anger I would sleep better, eat better, have improved relationships with family, do better at work or school?

8. What are some reasons to let go of the anger?

Forgiveness helps you move on from the past, live for today and build your future.

© 2012 SMART Recovery® - All Rights Reserved

Forgiveness is a Process

The Process of Forgiving: Like other types of behavior change, the "act of forgiving" is a process and not an event. It starts with a conscious choice, followed by intentional action to change your thinking about your Loved One (LO) and their actions.

Decide if Forgiving is in Your Best Interest

What outcome can you expect for yourself if you continue to focus on past hurtful events and your feelings of anger and resentment? Consider your answer to this question and the questions in the exercise *Exploring the Option of Forgiveness* in this section, to decide if you would like to entertain the idea of forgiveness as a strategy to improve your life.

Because anger can quickly become toxic, it may be helpful to remember that no one likes being with an angry, bitter or depressed person. Hanging on to past hurts not only interferes with your ability to be happy, it also gets in the way of your other relationships.

Define Forgiveness

One reason people sometimes have difficulty with forgiveness may have to do with how they define it.

Forgiveness is NOT the same as trust. Many people link forgiving with forgetting and think that forgetting is *required* in order to forgive. But this is not the case. We need to remember what has happened so that we can protect ourselves against further hurts. We can *forgive the person*, but we would do well to *not forget the behavior*. E.g., we might forgive someone for stealing, but we would be wise to lock up our valuables the next time they were around. We can forgive the person and accept the past behavior for the reality that it *is*. But because we don't forget, we learn that, until they show us otherwise, through consistent action, we would be wise not to trust others in matters where they have failed to be trustworthy.

Forgiveness is NOT about giving up our choice to work to make things better. Instead, forgiving requires giving up the wish to have had a different past and taking action to improve our life and our overall happiness in the present and in the future.

Forgiveness IS the act of letting go of anger and resentment. When we let go, we are able to think about past events without feeling the physical manifestations of anger and without feeling compelled to resort to unhealthy coping mechanisms like drinking, drugging, or disordered eating. When we let go, the past event becomes just one event in our life and no longer defines who we are.

Forgiveness IS an act of understanding — understanding that none of us is perfect and that we have all done things that we later regretted.

Work to Understand Why Others Act as They Do

Develop new ways of thinking about your LO. Work on seeing his point of view. Recognize that his actions made perfect sense to him at the time, given what was going on in his life.

Let Go and Move On

Forgiving is hard work. Although your anger might seem justified, at some point you have to ask yourself, "What kind of person am I, and what is my anger doing today?" Are you a person who wants to remain a bitter, angry victim? Do you want to continue spending your time thinking about how you were hurt and how unfair it was? Take a good look at your anger, accept that what has happened is in the past, cannot be changed, and that remaining angry is *hurting you* more than anyone else.

> *"Forgiveness means letting go of a hurtful situation and moving on with your own happiness."* ~Amanda Ford

Start Small

If forgiveness as a strategy seems interesting but does not feel natural to you, you may want to begin by experimenting with practicing forgiveness in your daily life. For example, consider applying an attitude of forgiveness to those frustrating situations involving fellow drivers on your daily commute — or to fellow shoppers and fellow co-workers who behave in less than considerate ways. Work on recognizing that they had reasons that made their actions seem appropriate to them. As you become more comfortable with practicing forgiveness, allow yourself to extend the practice to include more personal situations.

Final thoughts

"Forgiveness means changing your mental, emotional, and behavioral reactions. When you forgive, you *think* in different, better ways about the life of the person who offended and angered you. You think about the forces that led that person to behave badly. Over time you begin to feel less anger when the problem comes into your consciousness, and you might even act to help the person who offended you in some way. We hope you'll consider forgiveness as a way of reducing your anger." *~Tafrate & Kassinove*

Adapted from: **Anger Management for Everyone,** *Tafrate & Kassinove*
Chapter 7: Forgiveness
http://goo.gl/yfSzci

> *"When I am able to forgive myself — which is not always easy —*
> *I am kinder to everyone. Including myself."* ~Sylvia Boorstein

 © 2012 SMART Recovery® - All Rights Reserved

Setting SMART Goals

In the book *Get Your Loved One Sober* (GYLOS), the authors stress the importance of choosing to shift your focus off of trying to fix the addiction. Instead, they encourage you to restore the balance in your life, to take care of your *whole life*, not just the current problems that you're experiencing because of the addiction.

There's a saying that if you don't know where you're going, any road will take you there. Wouldn't you rather *choose* where you're going? What do you enjoy that you've been missing out on lately? What would you like to see more of in your life? SMART goals are an excellent tool for planning how to regain lifestyle balance, how to get back in touch with those things you really value, and how to shift your focus back on to yourself.

S.M.A.R.T. Goals

Research indicates that the simple act of setting goals improves our experience and our performance. It also shows that we are happier when we are progressing towards our goals. Setting goals helps us focus on what we want.

When setting a goal, it can help to remember the acronym **SMART**.

SMART stands for: **S**pecific, **M**easurable, **A**chievable, **R**ealistic and **T**imed.

Specific

Your goal should be clearly defined. This gives you a direction to work toward. For example, setting a goal of doing more exercise is a bit vague. Setting a goal of going jogging every morning is much clearer and helps you to know exactly what you need to do. Include "What", "When", and "Where".

Measurable

Measurable goals give you a way to gauge your progress. When setting your goals, define "how much?", "how many?", and "how will I know when it is accomplished?" This will allow you to track your progress and refine your goals as needed.

Achievable

The goal needs to be something that you have the means to achieve. For example, if you set a goal of jogging 5 miles each morning starting this morning, but you are very unfit, you may be setting yourself up to fail. Remember it's your goal for yourself, not someone else's idea of what your goal should be. *Your* goal should be one that *you* are capable of reaching with a reasonable amount of effort.

Realistic

Try to make the goal within your means. You must have the opportunity and resources available to reach your goal. For example, if you hate jogging, then going jogging is probably *not a realistic goal for you.*

Timed

Each goal should have a time frame, whether it is a short-term or long-term goal. Having a deadline can help to avoid procrastinating. (E.g., "I'm going to start jogging as of next Monday and continue for three weeks, then reassess.")

"While wishes are great for birthday candles and falling stars, they don't help much in real life. You need to focus on specific behaviors if you want to see improvements." ~GYLOS

© 2012 SMART Recovery® - All Rights Reserved

Setting Goals

Often our Loved One's (LO's) addiction will seem to take over our lives. GYLOS emphasizes the importance of CHOOSING to shift our focus *off* the addiction and on to taking care of our *whole life*, not just the current problems that we're experiencing because of the addiction.

Obviously the relationship with our LO is important to us, but it is only one part of our lives. There are other things in a well balanced life that are also important. E.g., creativity, freedom, financial security, emotional security, leisure time, personal growth, food, shelter, safety. We are all different. You probably can think of other things in addition to this list that are important to you.

Setting goals to work toward can help to bring some balance back into your life. Most people have ideas about where they want to go in life and what they want to do, but many people don't achieve these goals because they lose sight of them or lack plans for how to achieve them.

Everyone has different goals. Following are some ideas for areas where you might like to set goals.

Study – starting or finishing a course, learning a new language

Creative/artistic – learning a musical instrument, joining a choir, painting, writing or gardening

Family – spending more time with a partner or children, seeing extended family more often

Work – changing careers, starting a new project

Friends – making new friends, spending more time with current friends

Financial – saving for a holiday or a car

Health – losing weight, developing an exercise routine, trying a new sport, taking up yoga

Home Improvements – doing home renovations, landscaping, building something

Spiritual – showing more compassion to yourself or others, learning to meditate

© 2012 SMART Recovery® - All Rights Reserved

SHORT-Term Goal Setting

Spend some time thinking about something important to you (separate from your relationship with your Loved One) that you would like to achieve in the short term (within the next 3 months). Use the questions below to clarify your goal and to plan your strategies for reaching it.

1. My Goal (Specific, **M**easurable, **A**chievable, **R**ealistic and **T**imed)

2. The most important reasons why I want to work toward this goal:

3. The steps I will need to take to reach this goal:

4. Some things that could interfere with reaching this goal (e.g., personal discomfort, resistance from others):

5. Possible solutions for things that could interfere:

6. How important is it to me that I reach this goal?

On the line below, mark **how important** this goal is to you.

Not important   *Very important*

0	1	2	3	4	5	6	7	8	9	10

7. How confident am I that I can reach this goal?

On the line below, mark **how confident** you feel about being able to reach this goal:

Not confident   *Very confident*

0	1	2	3	4	5	6	7	8	9	10

LONG-Term Goal Setting

Spend some time thinking about something important to you (separate from your relationship with your Loved One) that you would like to achieve in the long term (within the next 2 years). Use the questions below to clarify your goal and to plan your strategies for reaching it.

1. My Goal (Specific, **M**easurable, **A**chievable, **R**ealistic and **T**imed)

 2. The most important reasons why I want to work toward this goal:

3. The steps I will need to take to reach this goal:

4. Some things that could interfere with reaching this goal (e.g., personal discomfort, resistance from others):

5. Possible solutions for things that could interfere:

6. How important is it to me that I reach this goal?

On the line below, mark **how important** this goal is to you.

Not important										*Very important*
0	1	2	3	4	5	6	7	8	9	10

7. How confident am I that I can reach this goal?

On the line below, mark **how confident** you feel about being able to reach this goal:

Not confident										*Very confident*
0	1	2	3	4	5	6	7	8	9	10

© 2012 SMART Recovery® - All Rights Reserved

"Discover the Power of Choice!"

The SMART Recovery goal for Family & Friends is for you to achieve a healthy, positive and balanced lifestyle while supporting your Loved One (LO) in a meaningful and truly helpful way.

Our approach:

- ☼ Teaches self-empowerment and self-reliance
- ☼ Encourages individuals to change unhelpful habits and live satisfying lives
- ☼ Teaches tools and techniques for self-directed change

SMART Recovery advocates the *"power of choice"* and recognizes that each person's path of self-directed change is different. Throughout this Handbook, you've had an opportunity to explore many choices for self-empowerment, for self-reliance and for building a satisfying life.

This section explores the choices you've made, the choices you may yet wish to make, and how to move past fear in making choices.

With practice, patience and persistence, the tools in this Handbook can help you achieve a positive and balanced lifestyle which will enable you to more easily be a positive influence, encouraging your Loved One toward recovery.

Choices

The SMART Recovery approach emphasizes "empowerment" and *"the power of choice"* for those working on addiction recovery. As a family member or friend, we have the power of choice, too. We are not all-powerful, but we are far from power-*less*. Using SMART tools and CRAFT strategies, we learn:

> To manage our emotional upsets
> To change unhelpful habitual responses
> To challenge unrealistic and unhelpful thinking
> Effective ways to change and improve communication in the relationship
> The importance of healthy boundaries
> The importance of planning for non-drinking activities
> How to reward non-drinking behavior
> To work on developing our own support system
> To work on other ways to enrich our lives

Exercise – Choices

Take some time to reflect on how your attitudes and outlook have changed since you began to incorporate SMART tools and GYLOS strategies into your life.

What choices have you made for yourself, what tools have you used?

How effective have your choices been?

What has been helpful?

What hasn't worked?

What needs work?

What are some other tools or strategies that you'd like to implement in your life?

"Success is a journey, not a destination." ~Ben Sweetland

When To Quit?

The tools and strategies included in this Handbook support numerous life-enhancing skills: better emotional self-management, better problem solving and improved communications to name a few. These skills are all part of an emotionally healthy life and probably not something you will choose to quit.

With respect to your efforts to create lasting change in your relationship with your Loved One there may come a time when you question whether or not to continue those efforts.

Exercise – When to Quit

To help assess whether you have done everything that can be done in the situation, ask yourself the following questions:

_____Have I, as consistently as I could, mapped out problem situations and planned more effective, non-confrontational behaviors for myself?

_____Have I practiced a PIUS communication style?

_____Have I kept track of how my plans went and adjusted them based on those experiences?

_____Have I stopped acting as my Loved One's caretaker and allowed him to experience the real consequences of drinking/using?

_____Have I rewarded my Loved One for nondrinking behavior and made it as enjoyable as possible to be sober with me and/or the family?

_____Have I added pleasurable activities to my own life so that I am not totally absorbed by the drinking problems?

_____Have I figured out when the best windows of opportunity to suggest treatment are, and planned how I would use them?

_____Have I lined up a reasonable treatment option and made it available to my Loved One?

_____Is there anything that I thought might help and I meant to do but didn't?

_____Can I see an attractive future with this person?

_____Once I get over missing my Loved One, will a future without her bring me greater peace and happiness than one with her?

Reprinted from: **Get Your Loved One Sober,** *Meyers & Wolfe http://goo.gl/hTfQP*

Fear & Choices

FEAR: False **E**vidence **A**ppearing **R**eal

Often we put off making difficult choices out of fear — fear of what might happen as a result of our choice. This fear can keep us stuck, unwilling to make a change because we cannot guarantee the outcome of our choices. We become immobilized, effectively afraid of an outcome which has not yet happened and *which may not ever happen*.

> *"No passion so effectively robs the mind of all its powers of acting and reasoning as fear."* ~ Edmund Burke

Exercise – Resolving Fear

Divide a sheet of paper into three columns.

Column 1: What scares me? Name your fear or feared negative outcome. (E.g., I'm afraid if I leave, he'll just get worse.)

Column2: Write the fear as a "what if" sentence. What if that happens? (E.g., What if I leave and he does get worse?)

Column 3: What would I do in response? (E.g., I will feel guilty.)

Check in with yourself to see if actually confronting the fear and making a plan reduces the anxiety associated with it.

If it leads to another fear, such as feeling guilty, then make that the next fear in the first column and continue. Example:

1. I'm afraid he'll get worse and I'll feel guilty
2. What if I do feel guilty?
3. What would I do?

Keep going with this until you have a plan. This technique allows us to create plans for these feared outcomes (which may never come to pass). This gives us more control over them and reduces our worry about them. It takes away the mystery and allows us to reassure ourselves that if the feared outcome does occur, we will be able to handle it.

NOTE: This exercise can be used for any source of anxiety, not just anxiety related to making a difficult choice.

> *"Expose yourself to your deepest fear: after that, fear has no power, and the fear — shrinks and vanishes. You are free."* ~ Jim Morrison

© 2012 SMART Recovery® - All Rights Reserved Section 14: *"Discover the Power of Choice!"*

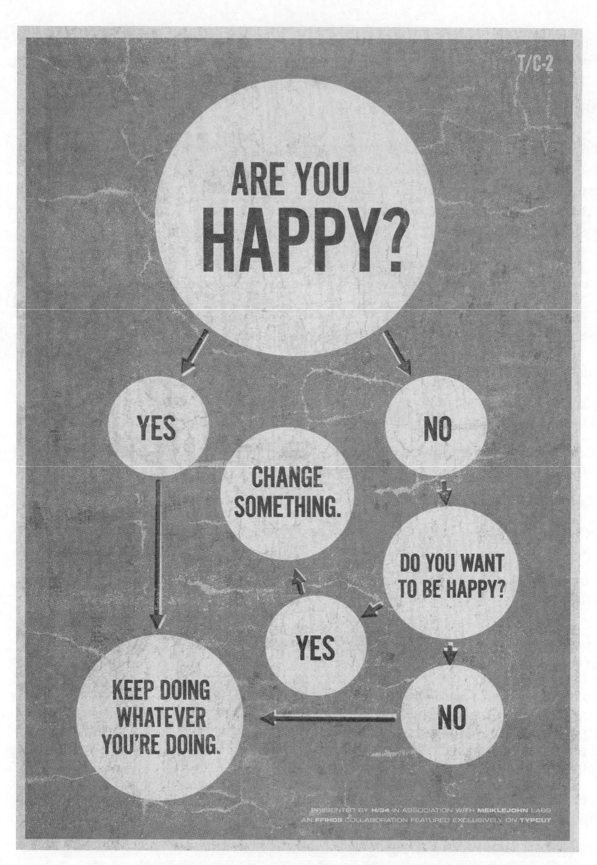

How to Be Happy © Alex Koplin and David Meiklejohn

© 2012 SMART Recovery® - All Rights Reserved

Appendix A – Suggested Reading List

Get Your Loved One Sober - *Alternatives to Nagging, Pleading and Threatening*
Robert J. Meyers, Ph.D and Brenda L. Wolfe, Ph.D

Beyond Addiction - *How Science and Kindness Help People Change*
Jeffrey Foote, Carrie Wilkens and Nocole Kosanke

I'm Right, You're Wrong, Now What? -*Break the Impasse & Get What You Need* Xavier Amador, Ph.D.

Anger Management for Everyone - *Seven Proven Ways to Control Anger and Live a Happier Life*
Raymond Chip Tafrate, Ph.D. and Howard Kassinove, Ph.D., ABPP

Boundaries -*When to Say Yes and How to Say No* Henry Cloud and John Townsend

Boundary Power - How *I Treat You, How I Let You Treat Me, How I Treat Myself* Mike O'Neil and Charles Newbold

Everything Changes - *Help for Families of Newly Recovering Addicts* Beverly Conyers

Loving an Addict, Loving Yourself
Candace Plattor, M.A.

Don't Let Your Kids Kill You - *A Guide for Parents of Drug and Alcohol Addicted Children*
Charles Rubin

Appendix B - Acknowledgements

The following sources are acknowledged as having been of assistance in developing this Handbook:

Amador, X. 2008, I'm Right, You're Wrong, Now What? - How to Break the Impasse and Get What You Need;, Hyperion, New York

Messina, J. J., Be-COS, Inc.; www.coping.us

Meyers R.J. & Wolfe, B.L. 2004, Get Your Loved One Sober - Alternatives to Nagging, Pleading and Threatening; Hazelden, Minnesota

Miller,W.R. & Rollnick S. 2002, Motivational Interviewing: Preparing People for Change ; The Guildford Press, New York

Steinberger, H. 2004, SMART Recovery Handbook; SMART Recovery Mentor, Ohio

Tafrate, R.C. & Kassinove, H. 2009, Anger Management for Everyone: Seven Proven Ways to Control Anger and Live a Happier Life; Impact Publishers, California

Be SMART: Family & Carers' Programme Facilitator's Manual; SMART Recovery, Australia

Menu of Options for Motivational Interviewing Exercises, 2009, UC San Diego, CCARTA

SMART Recovery Family & Friends Online Participants

© 2012 SMART Recovery® - All Rights Reserved